The Day I Didn't Kill Myself

Proof there is life after divorce,
depression and suicidal thoughts

DebS

Dedication

*To my wonderful mum who has been an inspiration
and is always in my heart.*

Michelle

Thank you for your assistance
in helping bring this book into the
public domain.

Much appreciation

Debs

x

Contents

Preface 1

Prologue..4

Divorce 7

Depression, Denial, Doctor 16

Dazed, Devastated, Desperate....................32

Digging Deep and Divine Interventions ...39

Discovery, Development, Decisions..........57

From Singledom to Soulmate 81

Dearth and Death...................................... 100

Delightening... 137

Epilogue... 145

Thank You.. 157

Free Gift 160

Further Inspiration 161

About the Author... 162

Preface

This is my story. It relates how I recovered from a time of being at rock bottom where I was lacking in self-worth and self-confidence and tells how I became the woman of strength, empowerment and full of self-love and self-esteem that I am today.

This is the story of how I woke up to the understanding that life sends us lessons to test us and to see how strong we are. This is the story of what I discovered about myself but also of what worked for me and what helped me to be where I am today.

Words are very important to me and they have been a huge part of my journey, from words in my head to my poems and now the words I have written in this book.

This is my story, my journey of self-discovery: from divorce through the depths of depression to "delightening" (and yes, I have made this word up).

This is the story of how I discovered that not all trauma means the end of the world, as I believed it so back then.

This book is for anyone who is going through difficult, stressful, traumatic times and is for you if you want to find a different way of being or if you have been tempted to investigate holistic or "woo woo" interventions. This book is for those who are seeking change.

This book is a memoir, a self-help and poetry book all rolled into one. If you were drawn to it, then this book and these words were meant for you.

This is the story of me learning to love myself; of discovering and accepting myself, of loving my life in whatever shape or form any of that is.

I wrote this story as part of my own healing journey and I made the momentous decision to share it with the intention that it could inspire and empower you or assist you in some way on your own healing path.

I wrote it in gratitude for my journey and to celebrate that and to give thanks for life itself.

I hope that it makes you want to investigate a holistic journey into finding your best self; your own "*delightening*". It may release tears of sadness and tears of joy as it is written with honesty from my heart to yours. Whatever you feel about it, I hope it touches you and gives you hope and inspiration. If so, I consider my job to be done.

Much love, light, grace and blessings to you,

DebS x

Prologue

"Drive over the edge, go on drive off!
No-one's going to miss you!
Nobody cares! Nobody loves you!"

With no warning and out of nowhere, these words jumped into my head. I was travelling through the beautiful Brecon Beacons, the majestic mountains of Mid Wales.

In the peace and tranquillity of these surroundings, those words resonated, resounded and reverberated around my brain, screaming loudly, commanding and insistent. It was one of those surreal moments in life where time seemed to both slow down and speed up simultaneously. Tempted, I glanced down the steep, sharp drop… and I drove on.

I have no idea what date it was, nor the time, but what I do know is that it was "The Day I Didn't Kill Myself".

Beacons of Hope

The Beacons always beckon
Outside the town of Brecon
High mountains for some to climb
Fresh air with no hint of grime
A sight for eyes that are too sore
Views that are "to die for".
A phrase too often used
Words I no longer abuse.
Because of my suicidal thought
A potential action I did abort.
With my depression I couldn't cope
Somehow the Beacons gave me hope.

Did the Beacons give me some element of their strength, power and magnificence? I'll probably never know. But what I do know is that I didn't take heed. I ignored that voice. I drove on across the Beacons. I kept going. Those words shocked me to my core. Those words were echoing around the empty chamber of my head… but I didn't drive off. Those words kicked me into action, not into touch. Those words made me realise I needed saving. Most of all, those words that arose unexpectedly from the depths of nowhere made me realise that I needed to get help, in order to help myself.

How my brain made that logical connection at a time when it felt as if it was barely functioning, I don't know. Did I have a guardian angel who lived in the Beacons or one that came with me everywhere I went? I have never been particularly religious, but I thank God or whatever energy it was that guided me to stay on that road.

Divorce

At the ripe old age of 35, I went through a bereavement; a separation, a loss. But my husband hadn't died – we were getting divorced. We had what was called an "amicable divorce".

Regardless of the term used, I learnt later that it was akin to a bereavement in that it was an ending that invoked many of the emotions of a bereavement. It was, however, without the finality of anyone having passed away, which clearly is the ultimate bereavement. It meant losing the whole of my future as I thought it was going to be; losing my home, my best friend, my lover and my companion. I lost all this, and I, myself, was lost. I never realised I was so fragile; it shattered my heart and broke it into pieces. It broke me. I was broken.

Broken

She put down her pen.

Her hand shook like a dried-up old leaf, hanging by a thin stalk at the end of a branch.

A single tear slid down her face and splattered onto the paper, spreading and diluting the ink like a blood stain.

Her shoulders shuddered.

Her breath ragged.

Snot poured from her nose as the lonely tear became a torrent when she realised the letter was unfinished.

She struggled to read over what she had written.

Was it the tears blurring her vision or the content that made it difficult?

Her trembling hand picked up the pen and wrote one more line:

"Why don't you love me anymore?"

This ending broke her and the stark realisation shattered her heart into pieces.

She dropped to the floor and sobbed until empty.

The slate floor felt as cold as her heart.

Her nerve endings rubbed raw and hyper-sensitive.

Her body felt numb.

Her mind emptied of all thought.

Her being finally devoid of all feeling.
The silence crept up around her and shrouded
her in its oppressive, heavy cloak.
Slowly, stiffly she rose.
Diverting her eyes from the paper and pen,
blindly she looked ahead to the door.
She gathered her paltry belongings and stumbled
away from uncertainty and into the unknown.

———————————————————————

Allow me to set the scene for you. I had been with my boyfriend since I was 21. We met at polytechnic, then lived together and got married within the space of two to three years. In our early years, we lived in a town, in a house with no garden. We didn't really have any choice as it was all we could afford. I'm a country girl at heart. I love green hills, fields, mountains and wide-open spaces with lots of light and big skies. I was happy in my work, and I thought I was happy at home too.

Unfortunately, my own workplace friends all lived a minimum of a 30-minute bus journey away, so there was no-one I could just pop and see for a coffee or a chat. We didn't have a landline in the house, and we certainly didn't have mobile phones back then. I didn't realise it at the time, but I was lonely. The house was old and, to me, always seemed dark and felt cold. My husband was working all hours to complete his professional exams, and I had a full-time job I enjoyed. We were both working hard for our future to be better. I'm not sure what I expected, and certainly, on the surface, I felt happy with my lot and he seemed to be too. I was oblivious, though, to the hidden discontent that was rumbling away in the background.

We didn't have children, a decision I ultimately made but that he was happy with at the time we discussed it. Eventually, we achieved our goals of a lovely, detached house with a gorgeous garden in a nice semi-rural area; a holiday abroad every year; a car each; we had our sport and fitness interests and a group of friends from poly we saw regularly. We laughed a lot and had fun. So what went wrong? That is the $64,000 question. I have gone through this with a fine toothcomb. I thought I had everything, so why did I feel unfulfilled, discontent and dissatisfied on some level? To this day, I still really don't know. Perhaps this is a pattern in the modern western world? We hear of lottery winners who end up miserable; celebrities with fame and fortune who turn to drugs or alcohol; they appear to have everything, yet on some level are also dissatisfied and unhappy.

What I do know is that there was a point where I came to the realisation that he no longer loved me. I say this as if it was a quick decision. I highly doubt it. I think it was something that had been creeping up unawares over the years, but there was one incident that suddenly hit me over the head like a huge heavy iron hammer. It seems the *coup de foudre* that got us together became the bolt of lightning that split us apart.

One day I returned home having been to see the doctor. I walked into the lounge where he was sitting watching TV. There was no acknowledgement from him that I had even walked in, no concern about how I was. He didn't even look up from what he was watching. I might as well have been invisible. I felt like I didn't exist. I walked out, went upstairs and cried my eyes out.

Following this realisation, we tried to stay together. We tried for a few years. He tried. I tried. But it seems that we were never on the same page at the same time. Or perhaps we weren't trying hard enough? Or perhaps we were trying too hard? It was energy-sapping. Looking back, I now realise that underneath it all, I wasn't content. I had put on weight and felt unattractive and sluggish. On some level, I wasn't satisfied with myself or the life I was living, and I clearly didn't love myself.

Please remember that this is my story, and every story has at least two sides, and this is my perspective, seen through my eyes only. I have my theories, and I had my instinct. I did, however, discover by accident many years after our divorce that my instinct had been proven to be right, that he did no longer love me, and I had actually made the right choice to walk away. I say it as if it was an easy decision. Absolutely not. It was the hardest decision I have ever made in my life. My heart felt leaden and heavy with hurt, wracked with regret, guilt, doubt, fear and my head was full of "what ifs" and riddled with disappointment and uncertainty. It was such a monumentally difficult decision that I left and returned twice before leaving for good. Once for a day, then for a weekend and then forever.

Even then though, we carried on seeing each other, still bound by some invisible thread of non-acceptance of the situation or were we just scared and full of fear for our new futures that bore no resemblance to the futures we had envisaged when we met, fell in love and got married? I don't know. I felt I didn't know anything back then, other than I truly believed that he no longer loved me like he used to and that on some sub-conscious level, I deserved better.

One thing I am proud of to this day is that we never played the blame game. On some instinctive level, I knew that we both had our part to play, and I chose to believe that neither of us was to blame. It suited me to believe that we had just drifted apart. There seemed to be no other explanation. Had we become complacent and taken each other and our lives for granted? I don't know, and to this day, I still don't know. At the time, my logical mind kicked in. I wanted reasons;

I wanted to know why. What was the matter with me? What had I done wrong? Was I too boring or too fat? Why did I think he stopped loving me? It was like an "earworm" wriggling around in my head day in, day out. The words wouldn't leave me. They were echoing through the chambers of my mind constantly. *Why? Why? Why? Why? Why?* It was like an insistent child badgering an adult for answers or a woodpecker constantly trying to bore a hole in my head, like a record stuck in a groove with the same words repeating incessantly. Whatever the analogy – it was driving me insane.

Whys and Wherefores

Why did we fall out of love?
Why did the hand no longer fit the glove?
Wherefore did we drift apart?
How could he break my heart?
Where did it all go so wrong
After being as one for so long?
Questions that needed replies
Not found, as we said our goodbyes.

It haunted me for years and was probably a huge factor in the depression that ensued from our break-up. This need to know why, this over-analysing, became one of the greatest challenges I had to overcome in my recovery from depression. I have had to learn to let go of needing to know why things happen or why people behave in certain ways and to just go with the flow, to be more accepting and stop fighting the tide. But where would this tide wash me up?

Depression, Denial, Doctor

And so, back to the Beacons and that suicidal thought.

The rest of the journey was a blur. I don't remember much other than a feeling of shock at having had those words appear. A voice in my head suggested that I should attempt to kill myself, that I should commit suicide by driving off the road and if I did, that no-one would miss me because no-one cared or loved me.

Those words rocked the very core of my being, and perhaps that shockwave could have released some strength. The shock of it must have brought me to my senses in some way, a bit like a defibrillator does when someone's heart breaks down; it literally shocks it back to life.

It shook me energetically yet somehow invoked a resilience. It must have released something in me because my subsequent thoughts were that I needed to get help. This was a huge first step to learning to love myself. I was saying to the Universe that I was worth saving.

I believe my heart had broken down. I know it had suffered an attack, not of the physical kind but of the emotional kind. It had an emotional breakdown which subsequently led to a mental breakdown. For me, depression was an emotional breakdown that also had physical and mental, as well as spiritual and energetic connotations. I was no longer whole but in a hole. I deem depression to be a holistic breakdown because, for me, it involved the whole of my being, and ironically it was a holistic approach that helped to mend me and my heart. I believe what got me through was a holistic mix of allopathic medicine, natural medicine, talking therapies; energy therapies and animal therapy, all bound together with love therapy from my parents and friends.

None of my senses were working. I was totally in automatic mode. I don't remember what I felt like, what sort of day it was – I don't remember any detail, but somehow I made an appointment to see my GP. She was a lovely lady with a holistic outlook, whose dog was always in the room with her and who, on the few times that I had met her, always struck me as if she had a light shining from within. When she asked me the question: *"So what seems to be the problem?"* I told her about how I had been feeling: numb, isolated, lonely, lost, sad and low, and then I started sobbing – I broke down. In between sobs, I somehow managed to ask for details of a self-help group so that I could sort myself out.

"And what about the depression?" she asked.

"Depression? What depression? I'm not depressed, just a bit low, a bit down."

Talk about being in denial. I had probably been in denial for quite a while. Until the shock of those words jumping into my head, urging me to drive over the edge of the mountain, I hadn't wanted to help myself; I didn't even know that I needed help, and I certainly didn't know how to do it.

My doctor officially diagnosed me with depression. I think the fact that I received this diagnosis gave me permission to be depressed; to allow it out; to allow it to show. Please don't get me wrong here, I'm not blaming her. In fact, I'm grateful otherwise, I probably would have kept pushing it down and eventually imploded.

She gave me tablets. I didn't want tablets. Bear in mind that back in the '90s and prior to that, mental health wasn't talked about like it is now. It wasn't discussed openly or admitted to; it was something to hide, to be embarrassed or ashamed of.

I told the doctor that I didn't want tablets, I just wanted details of a self-help group, and I would be alright. She looked directly at me and asked me whether I trusted her. Inexplicably I did - implicitly. She told me that if the circumstances were reversed, she would definitely take what she was prescribing for me. I trusted her. I collected the tablets, but by the time I reached home, I had decided I wouldn't take them, that I would be fine, that I could do this myself; I didn't need any tablets! My mum, though, had other ideas. She rang me for an update, and she threatened to come down and make me take them if she didn't hear me take them over the phone. So I took them.

Around this time, my first poem appeared. When I say appeared, that's exactly what I mean.

It appeared in my head like those words suggesting I kill myself had. I was staying with Mum and Dad, and it came in the middle of the night or the early hours of the morning. I felt guided to write the poem down, and the words flew out of my pen. They felt like a download from somewhere else, bypassing my brain as if from some other part of me - such a similar scenario to how that suicidal thought appeared. The poem came out in its entirety, fully formed, almost a full A4 page of rhyming couplets.

At that time, nothing made sense. My brain felt like it had shut down. It felt as if it had lost all its thinking power, all its rational logic abilities. It seemed only able to cope with the very basics. My understanding from the doctor was that in depression, the neural pathways in the brain are disconnected, and the chemicals can't jump over the gaps (synapses), so the messages don't get through. This might explain why certain thoughts don't make sense, are illogical and, in actuality, untruthful. Also, in a state of shock, trauma or stress, all the blood rushes to the back of the brain to enable you to be ready to run, fight or freeze.

This means that the thinking part of the brain at the front isn't getting the blood it needs to make rational decisions.

Whether it is because of this or as a result of this or some other reason, somehow I made a connection that I was clearly and obviously completely unlovable. After all, if my husband, the man I was supposed to spend the rest of my life with, didn't love me, then who else would? Despite this, as you can see from this poem, on some level, I must have felt a deep sense of love still being directed to me from my mum and dad, for which I was clearly grateful.

I Don't Understand, But Thank You Anyway!

For all the trouble that I cause
You're always there without a pause
But then you've been there right from the start
with love and support straight from your heart

How can I have been so very lucky
to have two such parents, both so plucky?
I'll never be able to say thank you enough
'Cause I find talking these days really quite tough!
I don't want to burden you with all my woes
And I'm scared to disappoint you from your head to
your toes
I really don't think I come up to scratch
I'm no use to anyone - not even to Patch!*
I feel that I've failed you, this only daughter of yours;
no husband, no grandchildren; not even the chores
get done anymore as I'm in quite a state
It's really all down to something called hate.
A hate for myself, for the way that I am
Always me first until I'm in a jam.
I know it's not right to put myself first
but lately I feel like I'm going to burst
into tears all the time and then it subsides.
My life's a roller coaster that's no fun to ride.
At the moment I know that I'm down in a dip
I know this for sure, there's a trembling lip
never far from appearing - oh where is the smile
that used to be on me more than once in a while?
I know that I need to get myself out
of these present doldrums and stop this last pout.
It helps to know that you're always so near;
it helps to take away some of my fear.

My routine, my life has irrevocably changed
I don't know where I am; it's addled my brain.
I have to get up and dust myself down,
Lighten my spirits, smooth away my frown.
I need to regain the focus and vision
I had months ago when I made some decisions.
And while I'm like this, in the background
there you both are, patiently waiting around
offering help and support, but most of all love
I feel it around me, slipping on like a glove.
And I want you to know more than anything else
this works the other way round. The love it is held
in my heart for you too, though it doesn't oft' show
it's always been there, always will.......So
if you ever need me, please let me know
I'll be there like a shot, an arrow from a bow.
You're always so giving and I want to give back
I'm just searching to see if I've still got the knack.
Just 'cause I don't ring, doesn't mean I don't think
of you both very often. There's always a link
between you and me until we all die,
this wondrous love, this unbelievable tie.

---

* *Patch was our lovely but daft family rescue dog.*

Despite the doctor telling me that the tablets were fairly mild anti-depressants, they initially made me very ill. I was physically sick for almost two weeks, and they invoked an episode of paranoia. The paranoia was so bad I remember feeling extremely scared and panicky that if I left the house, everyone would be looking at me because everyone would know I was depressed and ill. I thought people were watching me through my window. I wouldn't even go out into the garden. I was panicky, scared, sick and alone - so what did I do? I phoned my husband. I didn't know what else to do. I needed someone there and then. I had never felt anything like this before, and I was scared. Thankfully I have never felt like this since. In all fairness, he came over and calmed me down. I don't remember how. I don't remember him coming or going or what he did or said. I am just grateful he came. If I had been thinking in any way clearly, I would have thought that at least he cared enough to do that. I couldn't even think. Logic isn't a normal symptom of depression.

Depression can be a vicious circle – it's definitely a circle that is vicious. I realise it's not the same for everyone. For me, I felt extremely low and lacking in energy, and so desperately miserable all the time. I just about managed the basics. On some days, I didn't get up; others I did. Some days I did have a shower; others I didn't. Toast and cereal became a wonderful quick, easy meal. Lacking in nutrition and therefore energy and making poor food choices resulted in erratic sleep patterns, which then created a lack of energy, and so that vicious circle came round again. Lack of sleep and lack of energy invoked negative thoughts, and negative thoughts created poor choices, and so it came round again - a downward spiral of negative thinking and getting stuck in a vortex or spiral of doom and gloom.

Depression was something to be ashamed of. Depression was something that wasn't talked about openly. Depression was hidden because it wasn't physical. It was mental. Depression was something to be kept secret. Depression caused me to experience chaotic, unhinged, illogical thinking. My husband didn't love me; therefore, how could anyone else? It certainly didn't lead me to realise that the deeper question should have been that if I didn't love myself, then how could I expect him or anyone else to? Depression didn't let me see further than the end of my own nose. Depression for me was self-centred, destructive and an extremely negative place to find myself in. When I did think, all I could think about was myself and how bad I was feeling, how low I had got, and when would the flow of tears stop. Most of the time, I was numb. The anti-depressants exacerbated this dulling of my senses; not only did they numb the pain, but they also numbed my mind and my emotions, too – both the good and the bad.

Black Hole

I fell into a black hole
That made life feel so unfair.
It sucked me in and swallowed me up
Into this vortex of despair.

Smothered by a blanket of fog
I was rendered blind
Lost with no obvious exit route
Blankness engulfed my mind.

My eyes had but one function
Torrents and streams of tears
No "in", "fore", or "hind" sight
I couldn't see beyond my fears.

It caught me unawares
Denial, its blindfold mask
Stalked me until I fell
My downfall its only task.

Jumping into my head
That day appeared a voice
Urging me to kill myself
It didn't offer me a choice.

I fell into a black hole
Of complete and utter suppression.
It sucked me in and swallowed me whole
Into this vortex called depression.

———————————————————————

It's interesting how different an experience depression is for each individual who experiences it. Matt Haig said in his book, *Reasons to Stay Alive*, that: '*Depression, for me, wasn't a dulling but a sharpening, an intensifying, as though I had been living my life in a shell and now the shell wasn't there.*' Yet I felt empty, I felt dull, I had my shell but felt hollow inside.

I am convinced, though, it was because of this emptiness, this empty space inside me, inside my brain, this hollowness, that my poems were able to emerge, to be born, to flow forth. Perhaps because I was now an empty hollow vessel, instead of a busy human "doing", there was space for them to appear? I had been forced to become empty, but maybe this was a silver lining to the black cloud that hung over me? I believe this emptiness allowed the words to flow and that in itself was clearly part of the healing process, despite it not being obvious at the time. This particular poem expressed how sorry for myself I was feeling.

Sorry For Myself

Does anyone care except my mum and my dad?
Does anyone care that I'm feeling so bad?
Does anyone know the misery inside
That engulfs me so often, I can't cast it aside?
They're all too busy to care a jot
All too cocooned to worry a lot
About little old me and what I've become
An outer, a kernel, a casing, a shell
No insides, so hollow - feeling like hell!
No future, no past, not even a present
A burnt-out body with many a dent
All I want is someone to share
My life, my future - just someone to care!

I was on sick leave for a while, living on my own and crying all the time (well, it felt like all the time). I remember thinking that surely there was no water left inside me, but still the waterworks came. I couldn't listen to music, watch telly or read books. I didn't want to go out, speak to anyone or see anyone. I was constantly feeling sorry for myself. Looking back, it was pitiful and pathetic. I was consumed by darkness and negativity; there was no room for love, light, hope, optimism or any other positive feeling.

I couldn't think about anything and felt I had nothing else really to think about. I truly believe it was this emptiness of mind, this lack of a busy brain, this numbness of emotions, this feeling of being frozen in time, this vast space that opened up in my life that allowed the poems to flow through because it was when I was at this lowest point that I first started receiving poems. I say "receiving" because they seemed to come through me, not from me. And what's more, they always came fully formed and in rhyme. This was such a surprise as I hadn't shown any inclination to write poetry (if my rhymes can be classed as that) before. I don't remember ever studying poetry in English at school and I studied English for 7 years. I'm sure we must have had poems on the curriculum, but I certainly didn't have any predilection for writing poetry or recollection of writing any in school. Mine seemed to come through me as if they had bypassed my brain. They still arrive like this to this day when I give them space to.

Being severed from my future hopes, expectations and dreams not only brought on depression, but also a feeling of being dazed and concussed. It felt like I was just going through the motions of life without noticing anything. I have huge parts of that time that I don't remember but what I do know is that the tablets gradually did their job and gave me the strength to return to work. I don't know how I managed to do my job, but I did… somehow. Perhaps because I had been doing it so long, it was relatively easy, and I think I functioned on automatic pilot most of the time. I was just about keeping my head above water, but underneath I was drowning. Would I sink, or would I swim?

Dazed, Devastated, Desperate

This has been the most difficult chapter to write because it is a part of my life that I am ashamed of and that very few people know about. In fact, I am disgusted with how I behaved at times during this dark period. I do not recognise that person who I became back then. I had lost my anchor, and as a result, I was set adrift, and the consequence was that I felt like I was drowning. I had no rock to cling to, no rudder to keep me steady. I was depressed and in a very deep dark hole, so when a light was shone on me, I bathed in it because it felt like the sunshine had been switched on.

This resulted in me having a few "inappropriate relationships", and I am NOT proud of this. They used to be called affairs, but I am calling them "inappropriate relationships" because that is exactly what they were. Anyway, whatever they are called, I am writing about them because this is a huge part of my recovery and my learning about life, and it was real and may resonate with you.

I reiterate that I was ashamed of who I was back then. Each time I was shown some attention, I thought I was being loved. My emotions had become so mixed up and so out of kilter I did not know myself or recognise which emotions were which at all. I thought I was in love, but I was actually in need. I had become needy (or had I been needy all the time and hadn't realised it?). I was in need of an anchor, of attention and of adoration. I couldn't see that I had become a user and that I was also being used. Each character had their own part to play in this pathetic chapter of my story, but I was needy and greedy for "love", and I ate hungrily. I got sucked in and revelled in the attention. I felt amazing in the moment, but the highs of relationships like these are matched equally by the lows of subterfuge and the restrictions. The highs are addictive, and the lows are devastating.

I didn't plan to have any "inappropriate relationships". Let's face it, I could hardly plan my dinner, let alone anything else. Looking back, though, I feel like I must have had the words "devastated and desperate" and perhaps even "mug" etched on my forehead for all men to see. I certainly seemed to be attracting men from all walks of life. I was lost, lonely, confused, dazed, devastated and desperate. This chapter of my life is a mistake I do not intend to make again. The fall-out to others is too costly. I do care very much about other people, but back then, all I cared about was getting myself out of the dark suppressive cave I was in and back out into the sunshine where I could breathe again.

After almost 15 years of love, care and attention and being the centre of someone else's world and then having that taken away, I craved it again. I needed to feel loved, cared for and wanted by someone, anyone! Yes, I needed to be wanted, and I wanted to be needed. I needed someone who just wanted to be with me, and I was prepared to accept pretty much any crumbs because I did not love myself. I didn't realise I was looking for love in the wrong place: externally instead of internally. So, when someone else did show me love (aka attention), I grasped at it like it was a survival raft. As I said, it was like someone shining a torch into the darkness of my life and lighting up the area around me. The problem is that torch batteries eventually run out, and that particular light then dies. My light had died, but what I didn't know then was that I was looking for someone to reignite it, to turn my light on, to do it for me. If I'd known then what I know now, I could have turned my own light back on, and all that emotional angst and upheaval could have been avoided.

In some ways, though, I did benefit from this "false love" and attention, from being made to feel as if I was wanted, regardless of the circumstances. It soothed my ego, but it didn't mend my heart. I know I wanted more than I was being given, and as a result of that, I was on the receiving end of many broken promises, which gradually wore me down, but also woke me up and opened my eyes to the reality of the situation.

With the help of the tablets, I gradually became stronger and able to cope with living day by day. I had to dig deep to manage, but I was also starting to wake up to life again generally. It started to dawn on me that my latest relationship wasn't based on love, so it was extremely unhealthy. This was using and neediness. Promises made were empty, and the relationship wasn't "normal". There was no going out for meals or meeting friends together, or speaking on the phone whenever we wanted to. Realisation slowly gathered pace that this was a destructive type of relationship and one that I no longer wanted to be part of. I began to learn that I deserved better than this. I was taking more steps towards self-love.

It took a while, but don't forget that my brain wasn't fully functioning at the time, and the tablets had a numbing effect on my emotions. I believe that I could only sense the intense, heightened feelings, the extreme highs and lows but not the milder ones in between.

As I became stronger emotionally, a glimmer of self-worth started to emerge. It dawned on me just how unhealthy and one-sided these "relationships" were and that I actually deserved better, and so did their partners and their families. Despite the part I had played in this, I began to understand that it was wrong for me and everyone else involved. I ultimately knew that it was time to say "goodbye" to that chapter of my life. This is a poem that came to me at the end of my longest "inappropriate relationship".

Goodbye

Well I have to say, it's been the best
But it's also been the worst
And now the chips are really down
It's me you choose to hurt.
I think this time is a bridge too far
This straw broke the camel's back
I'll always be "the one that got away"
The train you couldn't keep on track.
In a way I'm glad it's over
This awful waiting game
So now I can get on with my life
Though I think it's a crying shame.
So I want to proffer my thanks
I'd like to propose a toast
To you and I – not us – you see
"We" never existed, purely ghosts!
Although the words aren't' easy
I think now we both know

"Parting is such sweet sorrow"
But it really is time to go.
So here it is, the time has come
The moment we've both been dreading
Goodbye to you and thanks, my love
To our futures, separately, we're heading.
We really must say "au revoir"
And inside my heart I sigh
For it's in agreement with my head
It's really time to say goodbye.

_____

Over time I learnt that I didn't need to receive validation through other people's love. I wanted it and had craved it, but need - no! I have come to understand over the intervening years that the most important thing is to give love to ourselves first. When we do that, it's like charging up our own batteries and turning on our own inner light so that we then have plenty to give others; genuine heartfelt love, not head-felt love – it's so empowering. Giving pure, beautiful, unconditional love from our own hearts to ourselves first and also to others is such a gift. I was learning how and I was definitely getting there. But where was "there"?

Digging Deep and Divine
Interventions

In addition to the anti-depressants, my doctor had referred me to the practice counsellor. However, I doubted the counsellor was going to be able to help me one bit. How wrong I was. (I should explain here that I was completely disillusioned by a Relate counsellor I saw during the time that my husband and I were "trying" when she suggested that my husband might be gay! So perhaps you can understand my reservations?)

Not only was my GP an open-minded holistic lady with a heart of gold, but my counsellor was cut from the same cloth. We hit it off straight away, and I started to open up. I talked, and she listened. I felt heard. It felt wonderful to have someone to divest myself of my deepest fears and feelings. It felt amazing to offload to someone who seemed to totally understand what I was going through; someone with empathy and consideration for my situation, but someone who was neutral too, someone who didn't want to fix me but to just let me talk. I didn't offload to my friends or family because I thought that just by me being in their presence would drag their energies down.

I think it is easier for women to talk about their issues than it generally is for men, but as I've said, depression wasn't something that was openly talked about by anyone, no matter what gender. In *Reasons to Stay Alive,* Matt Haig said it took him more than ten years to be able to talk openly about his experience of depression and that he soon discovered that "the act of talking is in itself a therapy" and "where talk exists, so does hope".

It didn't take me as long as ten years, but when I did eventually talk about it with chosen people I trusted, I was both amazed and shocked to hear that many others had also suffered from depression and were on or had been on anti-depressants. It definitely helped to discover that I really was not alone when depression felt so isolating.

With my counsellor, I had struck gold. This lovely lady played a huge part in my recovery and my discovery of self. I do believe that she was heaven-sent. She helped me make sense of what I was going through and to understand why I was behaving like I was by seeking love and attention from anyone. But it was more than that. For instance, she gave me a copy of the following poem by an anonymous author, which really resonated with me. Perhaps this ignited a spark for me writing poetry? I'll never know, but I kept a copy of this on the wall for a very long time. Who knows what depths of my psyche these words touched.

Don't Quit

When things go wrong as they sometimes will
When the road you're trudging seems all uphill,
When the funds are low and the debts are high
And you want to smile, but you have to sigh.
When care is pressing you down a bit,
Rest if you must, but don't you quit.
Life is strange with its twists and turns
As every one of us sometimes learns

And many a failure comes about
When he might have won had he stuck it out.
Don't give up though the pace seems slow…
You may succeed with another blow.
Success is failure turned inside out
The silver tint of the clouds of doubt.
And you never can tell just how close you are,
It may be near when it seems so far.
So stick to the fight when you're hardest hit
It's when things seem worst that you must not quit.

Anonymous

I started to feel more positive generally through counselling, and I became more aware of the role that I had to play in my own life. I still had down days, but the down days were decreasing, and the up days were increasing. I found my poems were less dark, intense, miserable and full of self-pity but were beginning to show signs of hope

As I previously mentioned, my counsellor was holistically minded, and she also practised meditation and told me about something called

Reiki healing. From being frozen and numbed off emotionally and mentally, now I started to open like a flower, my petals unfurling one by one. I attended a Buddhist meeting but felt totally outside my comfort zone and very, very awkward, so I didn't pursue that but did, without thinking, incorporate some of the philosophies into my life. I liked the sound of Reiki and meditating, so alongside subsequently gaining a Diploma in Holistic Therapies, I trained as a Reiki practitioner and started listening to guided visualisations. These were stepping stones into a whole new world of love, light and healing. It was like being a kid in a sweet shop where I wanted to taste and try everything.

Another significant step forwards was being referred to a massage therapist who introduced me to vibrational medicine, dowsing and kinesiology/energy work. This man opened my eyes to alternative methods of healing, and he told me I was one of three people he was put on this planet to look after, which, when he said it, made me cry. He also took me to my first group meditation session, where I was surprised that my meditation journey was cartoonish and funny. As a consequence, I didn't speak up much during the feedback at the end as everyone else was saying how deep and spiritual it had been for them, whereas mine made me laugh. I believe now that I was given exactly what I needed at the time – some light-hearted entertainment. Even though he is no longer with us, I still truly appreciate his care and for looking after me when I needed it, which greatly contributed to my healing process.

I don't remember exactly why, but I felt drawn to investigate hypnotherapy and vibrational medicine further. It was from this point on that the events and reactions to them I had experienced started to really make some sort of sense.

The understanding I have gained is that everything affects us energetically, but the greatest effects are felt up to the ages of six or seven years old. We are not born with a manual for life, so everything is a learning curve. With the hypnosis training, we were taught that we are born with two main fears: the fear of loud noises and falling (or being dropped, perhaps?). But what about energetically? Does the energy of our mothers and fathers when they conceive transfer to us? Do our mother's feelings, emotions or events that happened to her get energetically transferred to us in the womb? Do the traumas of their parents and their parents' parents etc, get passed down energetically somehow too? As everything is energy, I believe this is not just possible but more than probable.

So what did this actually mean for me? What does this mean about the me I was back then? I believe we all have areas that contain strengths, memories, stories, beliefs, emotions, traumas, etc. Mine were hidden so deeply that it took the devastation of my life as I knew it being blown apart for more to raise their heads. I find it interesting that some people seem to get hit with one life challenge after another and find a super deep strength and resilience to keep going. Others, like myself, have a fairly blessed, ordinary, nice life where nothing much goes wrong, but when it does, they seem to have little or no resilience at all.

For me, two main incidents happened when I was young within the space of a few weeks that made everything go wrong. I didn't know this at the time, but my mum had mental health issues. She suffered from post-natal depression (or "baby blues" as it was called then) and one day it got too much for her. When I was six years old, she ran away and the police were called to help find her. My youngest brother was a baby, so she had taken him with her. I knew something was wrong because our next-door neighbour came to pick us up from school. I remember the kitchen door being closed. The kitchen door was never closed. I put my little hand on the handle and pushed it down. I opened it a fraction and could see a policeman sitting at our kitchen table with Dad, talking in low voices. The minute they realised I was there, they sent me out with some urgency. I burst into tears because I knew something was wrong. I wanted to know where Mum was. I felt confused and bewildered because she wasn't there. We were always allowed into the kitchen because it was the warmest room. It was where the Rayburn was, where we had our food; why wouldn't they let me in? I'm sure I must have had many more unanswered questions and fears. Why was there a policeman in the kitchen? Where was Mum? When was she coming back? I knew Mum wasn't there, and up to that point, she had always been there. I ran to my room, threw myself on the bed and cried, but no-one came to comfort me. Eventually, Dad came and held me, but he didn't know how to reply to my questions because perhaps he didn't have the answers.

I don't remember much of the interim period, but Mum did return, although she stayed in bed a lot. I wanted her to be better, to make her better, to hug her loads and to try to make her laugh to make her stay so she wouldn't go away again. I became very clingy. Unfortunately, this didn't work because the depression was so bad that not long after this, she tried to commit suicide by taking an overdose. She was taken away, initially to hospital and then to a sanitorium (as it was called back then). My older brother and I were told that Mum wasn't well and we were, thankfully, spared the details.

But within the space of a week, for the second time, my Mum had disappeared. All I knew as a young six-year-old girl was that my mum was no longer there… again! My world had been blown apart, again! My rock had been removed, again! My future was now uncertain, again! My life had been changed drastically, again! My stability had been shattered, again! My mum had gone, again! To me, as a little girl, this was bewildering, shocking and devastating.

We were well cared for by neighbours and friends, but Dad still had to go to work, and the bottom line was that Mum was NOT there anymore, and I didn't know whether she was coming back, and nobody seemed able to tell me.

I have since uncovered that the main feelings I had at that time were abandonment and rejection because the one person who I had the deepest connections with and who was supposed to love me the most in the world had disappeared. Of course, none of this was really true, nor anybody's fault, but as a young child with virtually no experience of life, the thought I created subconsciously was that it must have been my fault that Mum was ill, that she had gone. I was a child with no real awareness of the world and no manual to guide me, so I subconsciously created a belief which then became a pattern of fear of abandonment and rejection as a result of love being taken away, especially in the circumstances of my world being blown apart.

A poem appeared on a really dark day in May 2020, when I was examining the depths of my despair through a session with an EAM (Energy Alignment Method) Mentor. I realised that despite speaking about how I felt as an adult, I hadn't spoken about how I had felt as a child, and I believe this poem expressed the anguish caught up inside me. This poem made me feel like I'd given my little six-year-old girl a voice.

The Silenced Scream

Mouth open
Silent sounds
A disused dark tunnel
Agony inverted
Frustration stifled
Hurt quietened
Words swallowed down

Smothered and controlled
Jumbled thoughts
"I want my mummy!"
"Where's my mummy?"
Questions unanswered
Truth withdrawn
Fears embedded
Release valve failed
Pressure built
Eardrum burst
Nose bled
Jaw clenched
Teeth ground
Sick to the stomach
Nurture refused
Heart broken
Tears expressed
Voice repressed
Mouth open

THE SCREAM SILENCED

_____

I later learnt that the ultimate conclusion I
came to as a young child was that I must be
unlovable. I bet you're thinking, how on earth

could a young child create such a momentous belief? Well, when things happen without any logical explanation, our brains look for a reference point. My only reference point for the second incident was from the first incident. My young girl's brain wouldn't have been able to make any sense of this, so my logical brain decided that it must have been my fault and that if my mum could leave me, therefore I must be unlovable.

I may have had no manual, but I did have the previous story of Mum running away for my brain to refer to. I had emotions and beliefs from the previous event that resurged because even though the situation was different, the outcome was the same. This second trauma evoked the same feelings and belief patterns because the previous one was the only reference my subconscious brain had to check against. So the fears of an uncertain future, feelings of abandonment and rejection and a belief that somehow it must have been my fault, and I was therefore unlovable, were strengthened and became more fixed and permanent. Now I know that new negative neural pathways had been created.

This would eventually make sense of how I went so off the rails after being abandoned and rejected again later on in adult life when once more, love from the one person I thought should love me more than anyone else was removed. My rock again had gone, and my future again was uncertain. The situation was different, but the similarities of the circumstances were the same, and the subconscious negative beliefs that had been hidden away as a child, together with all those emotions, re-emerged stronger and more intense, as they were compounded by the emotions I then felt as an adult going through another life-changing, earth-shattering loss.

The trouble with negative energy, though, is that it has a stronger hold than positive. It lingers about hidden in the deep murky undergrowth waiting for you to be vulnerable. It's like a stalker, just waiting for the right time to catch you unawares when your defences are down. As I was growing into a normal hormonal teen and subsequently a young woman, they were lying dormant, deep down inside. They were hidden away under the optimism and hope of youth and young adulthood. All memories of the previous traumas pushed away with just getting on enjoying and experimenting with life.

So those were the negatives, but I guess I also learnt the positives, which were nearer the surface and therefore more accessible. Dad was still around, as were many friends who looked after us and cared for our basic needs. Dad's demeanour was always cheerful, optimistic and humorous; I don't think I can ever recall seeing him otherwise until the year before he died, and that was totally understandable considering his illnesses.

After Mum returned permanently, life eventually went back to "normal". I make it sound as if this was an easy time and it probably wasn't for Mum, but I feel like I subsequently grew up in what I mainly remember to be a happy household with lots of friends, fancy dress parties, holidays with family friends, playing outside, growing up with dogs and cats and just generally a good life. Happy memories, happy days, oblivious to the underlying deeply hidden emotional issues.

I want you to know that I have never blamed my mum or my dad for any of these events. They must have both made an enormous effort to make our childhood as happy as possible, and for that, I admire them and am grateful to them. They say children recover very quickly and I'm sure we did on the surface of it. I'm glad to say that my relationship with my mum has grown stronger over time, and I love her and admire her tenacity very much.

From my experience, I have concluded that I had to be emptied completely of everything; to have my existence blown apart, to have my rocks and anchors taken away so that I could find myself, to start again. All the other "life stuff" such as houses, jobs and material possessions are all pretty meaningless in the grand scheme of things, and many of us live with this superficial world around us. I wasn't mature enough to listen to the lessons or know I was even being given any at such a young age. I believe now, though, that each time my world was blown apart, I was learning. I was being given lessons, a positive learning of a blossoming blooming flower, while deeper down inside, the unknown negative weeds were growing hidden in the undergrowth.

As an adult, I have learnt that life throws us in all directions, but we can choose how we behave, what we say, what actions we take and what attitude to have. We may not always be able to choose what happens in our lives, but we can choose how we react and can influence our own mindset. Sometimes our lives are "all at sea", but could I really save myself?

A Life All At Sea

An analogy of life, that is the sea
The boats they are us and what we can be.
A tug, a tanker or a sleek yacht;
A lifeboat, a liner, a speed boat or what?
'Cause whatever we are, the sea governs us all
With its ebb and its flow, its waves hitting the wall.
So calm one day, so stormy the next
Is it really any wonder, we all get so vexed?
It tosses and turns us and moves us around
With eddies and whirlpools and undercurrents abound.

The tide takes us one way, but suddenly it turns
And backwards we go; will we ever learn?
Sometimes we must find ourselves a safe haven;
A lovely calm cove, our very own heaven
To relax and recuperate, to stop and weigh anchor
To recharge and unwind, to live life without rancour.
Until the sea and our lives, they beckon again
The challenge laid down, that same old refrain:
"Come out and conquer me"; the sea it does roar
"Don't cower and hide - like a seagull, just soar!"
So whatever the vessel - decide which you are
Ride with the waves and then you'll go far
Don't fight it or worry, don't let yourself drown
Look to the horizon - get rid of that frown!
For we all must learn to appreciate the beauty
Of the sea and our lives - I think it's our duty!

_____

Discovery, Development, Decisions

Building on these new understandings that I could choose my behaviour and responses, in addition to removing myself from damaging relationships and continuing with counselling, my general health and well-being slowly improved. I had been back at work for a while when I experienced another breakthrough moment. My department consisted of three men and a couple of women. We all got on really well, but the three men got on particularly so. They regularly bounced off each other and could be hilariously funny.

One particular day, all three were in the office and were on top form. I cannot to this day remember what set me off or what they were joking about; but they made me laugh. This may seem like an odd thing to highlight because laughter, to most, is a natural reaction to something funny. However, my experience of depression was that nothing seemed funny. The usual things that could make me laugh just didn't. I felt as if that part of me had been cut off and was no longer accessible. My giggle button had been switched off and my funny bones had disintegrated.

That day it seemed strange to hear my own laughter. It was as if some distant memory of it had flooded back. And this was proper belly laughter; laughter that came right from the very core of my body and hurt my tummy; that made me cry, feel weak and as if I was wetting myself. It felt as if all the laughter that had gone missing had been stored up inside, waiting for a chance to re-emerge. I recall thinking that I couldn't remember laughing like that for such a long, long time. That thought made me feel instantly sad, so whilst I was still laughing, I was simultaneously crying. They were tears of happiness and sadness at the same time, the two opposite ends of the spectrum working in unity and harmony for me. These tears, however, felt like a true release and gave me a newfound sense of relief as if a dam had burst. It was such a joyous moment.

Laughter is the "Bestest" Medicine

Oh my goodness, I've just had a laugh
A phenomenon archived away
Locked in a well of despair
Forgotten about until today.

A bewildering, delightful sound
Arose from the depths of my belly
It chuckled its way up into my mouth
My body wobbling around like a jelly.

My titter became a chuckle
Then a giggle that I couldn't stop
Which rippled through my whole being
From the bottom right to the top.

It continued until it hurt
My mouth and cheeks so wide
Tears streamed down my face
Tension loosened from the inside.

For a moment it subsided
As a sadness suddenly hit
A realisation of a lack of laughs
And then another giggling fit.

Sadness and gladness united
Crying and laughing together
A rush of released endorphins
Like being tickled by a feather.

The "bestest" medicine of all
A dose of laughter and fun
Tablets and capsules full of joy
My recovery had truly begun.

I realised that depression had numbed me off to having fun, laughing and enjoying myself. It felt like an underused muscle being brought back to life. It made me feel as if I had discovered some secret buried treasure. I felt as if I were rediscovering a part of me that had got hidden beneath the blanket of depression and despair. It was such a delicious discovery, and now it had returned this once, I wanted to experience it more often.

I believe this was another one of the turning points in my recovery – the re-discovery of laughter and the chain of happy hormones that it set off.

Things were starting to change due to that bout of laughter. It kicked off a chain reaction of new hope and emerging positivity. One thing, however, remained the same: the loneliness and reality of not having a companion at home. To combat this, I made the decision to go to evening classes: aromatherapy/reflexology, pottery, and I returned to playing badminton. This makes it sound incredibly easy, doesn't it? It wasn't. Apart from work I hardly went out. I avoided people because I didn't want to feel I had to explain why I was quiet, introverted, introspective, miserable, depressed, pale, listless, lifeless and devoid of emotion. I didn't want this different me to be on show. I felt conflicted between wanting more fun and company and wanting to stay wrapped up in my own cocoon of self-pity and despair. The pull towards the former option was greater than the latter, thankfully.

I chose these activities essentially to fill my time and avoid feeling like "Billy No Mates". After the initial feelings of self-consciousness in the first few weeks, I started to enjoy them. I had found my own stress relievers (but I hadn't studied the stress awareness course at that point, so I didn't actually know this). I was following my instinct and doing things that naturally felt good; they made me feel good.

Why did I choose these particular activities? I had always wanted to try pottery ever since the days of Bruce Forsyth's *Generation Game* which aired in the UK in the 1980s. It looked like so much fun, and the contestants had a proper laugh - and for me, it lived up to this in reality. The second term arrived and so did the moment of my dreams: being able to have a go on the potter's wheel. Oh my goodness, it was so much fun! Using my foot to press a pedal to spin the wheel whilst also trying to control a cold, sloppy, soggy piece of clay was like trying to catch a slippery, shelled, hard-boiled egg with wet hands. It was so much harder to do than it looked, but it was an absolute joy to try. I laughed so much, especially when what was intended to be an egg cup ended up as a tricorn hat or a mug became an ashtray. I did actually manage to achieve quite a few pieces that weren't too disastrous, and some looked halfway decent, but the most important thing was getting out of the house, being creative, meeting other like-minded people and at the same time, unexpectedly having fun.

My other evening class was aromatherapy and reflexology. I especially loved learning about aromatherapy oils and how they can help with various conditions. I was drawn to the citrus oils and discovered that they are uplifting. It was as if I naturally knew what I needed. I was starting to follow my intuition.

Around this time, I finished my counselling, and my lovely counsellor became a friend. She lent me a book called *The Celestine Prophecy*. It was a great read and a book that I still have on my bookshelf. A chapter I had been reading at the time introduced the idea of synchronicity and serendipity. Coincidentally, I kept seeing a poster from the local college advertising a Diploma in Holistic Therapies. But it was the fact that each time I read this poster, I got a warm, excited feeling in my belly. I didn't know what the course entailed, but my gut instinct was kicking in and I could feel it.

When I discovered that the course covered aromatherapy, reflexology and Swedish Massage, I really wanted to do it, but how could I? I was working full-time and living on my own, running a car but with very little money left over every month. Surely I couldn't go back to college; how would I manage? I discussed it with my holistic therapies evening class tutor, and she suggested I get a grant. I investigated this; however, there were no grants available to me.

I could not get this course out of my head and the excitement out of my belly every time I thought about doing it. I had virtually given up on the idea and decided I should stay where I was in a safe, steady, pretty well-paid job when someone suggested a Career Development Loan. I had never heard of such a thing, but it turned out that I could borrow enough money from a bank to fund the year I would be back in college. The beauty of it was that I didn't need to pay it back until I was in full-time employment again.

There was no guarantee I would be granted the loan, and also there was still the sticking point of paying for general day-to-day living expenses. Going back to college meant having to give up the safety net of my job in a place I had worked for 15 years, a place I felt safe, with people that made me laugh and with whom I enjoyed working. This was yet another huge decision for me to make, and I had to make it on my own. It felt overwhelming, and I didn't know what to do.

At this juncture, divorce proceedings were in progress. My husband and I were still, thankfully, talking to each other and had agreed that a two-year separation was the best solution. As he was previously my usual sounding board, and it affected me financially, I discussed this idea with him. To my surprise, his reaction was that he thought I should do it because I was always rubbing his shoulders or head.

Well, I did not see that coming, but I was surprised and extremely grateful. Perhaps this was my first real step onto the gratitude path? However, there was another hurdle. Due to the time it had taken to decide about the course and find out and apply for the Career Development Loan, I then had to make a quick decision about my job. I was contractually obliged to give a month's notice and avoid losing my place on the course. I needed to hand this in BEFORE I knew whether I had been granted the loan. If I didn't get the loan, I couldn't go to college, and I would have been out of a job as well. So to follow my heart and my instinct, I had to take a massive leap of faith.

I chose to jump and handed in my notice, and incredibly a day or two later, I received the letter saying that I had been granted the loan. What a relief! Was this a case of synchronicity? Who knows?

Read this explanation by Phil Cousineau and see what you think:

"Synchronicity is an inexplicable but profoundly meaningful coincidence that stirs the soul and offers a glimpse of one's destiny."

This was just the first of many synchronicities that have happened since then. It's a bit like "dripping tap syndrome": when you are made aware of something, you become more aware of it. (For those of you who don't know what "dripping tap syndrome" is, it's a term I coined when I was later working as a therapist to describe how we can be completely unaware of something, such as a dripping tap, until someone mentions it and then that's all you seem to be able to focus on or it's constantly playing on your mind in the background.)

Coincidence, fate, synchronicity, Law of Attraction, putting it out there, cosmic ordering - there are so many ways of saying pretty much the same thing. Whatever term is appropriate, it seemed that now I had started the ball rolling, and I was filling up my empty spaces with good energy, I noticed that synchronicity seemed to be having a domino effect. More kept coming my way. I was living in flow.

To explain more of these synchronicities, I need to back up a little bit in the story. Despite the Diploma being a full year, we weren't in college all day, every day. I had some time on my hands. Some of my time was now filled with teaching adults. (Yes, this is why I had to go backwards a bit.)

Do you remember me previously mentioning my evening classes tutor? Well, over the summer, she had been offered more teaching hours at the main college campus, and she knew that I was a bit financially strapped, so she suggested I apply for her existing job of running the evening classes. *Me? I can't teach; I've never taught.* She told me that she had never taught either, so surely if she could do it, then why couldn't I?

Her saying this, plus the fact she thought I could do it, gave me the confidence to try, so I sent my CV to the college. I didn't think for one moment that I would actually get the job. But I "went with the flow". Not only did I get that job, but they offered me additional hours teaching.

I said "yes". I didn't dwell on the fact that I had never taught formally before or how I was going to teach, or that I hadn't got any teaching qualification or experience. A practical incentive was that the extra income would be really helpful, and for that, I felt grateful. I had taken a leap of faith, and it paid off, another positive pattern that continued to repeat many times.

I have since discovered that taking these "leaps of faith" and "stepping out of your comfort zone" equates to placing "trust in the Universe" and I found that after I had done it once, it got easier and easier to do it again and again. Living life by going with the flow was so much easier than struggling, efforting, trying to control and fighting against life. I didn't know it then, but I was, in fact, creating new positive neural pathways in my brain.

This poem appeared when I was writing this book and looking back through this chapter in my life and realised that I had indeed taken several leaps of faith.

Leap of Faith

My life was being shaken up, right to the very core
One day a suicidal thought popped up. Would I go
through that dark door?
Well obviously I didn't, I chose a different portal
I went to the doctor for some help, to try and regain
my chortle.
This poem isn't necessarily in order because things
were all a jumble
My mind was all over the place yet underneath was a
steady rumble.
A rumble that became a roar, because finally I awoke
To listen to my intuition, to jump, to go for broke!
And when I did, I found more chances came my way
To jump a bit like hopscotch - the game I used to
play.
But this time I used two feet and legs and all the
power of trust
Girded my loins, looked into the abyss and with my
legs I thrust.
And so the moral of this poem; the tale I have to tell
Is, however scary it may feel, stepping outside your
cell

To care for your own future and show the Universe
that you trust
Take that leap of faith – I urge you, it's a must!

_____

Whilst studying for my Diploma in Holistic Therapies, I gained the requisite qualification to teach adults.   So I was teaching part-time, attending college part-time, yet still had some spare time on my hands. I was getting on with life and felt I was coming out of the doldrums when Mum suggested I get a dog. Without sugar coating it, she said that it would do me good to have something else to think about except myself as I had become "quite selfish and self-centred".

Only a mum or a very good friend can get away with saying things like that. I was lucky to have the two in one. But how could I look after a dog when I had only just learnt to start looking after myself again? My brothers and I grew up with dogs and cats, but Mum and Dad did all the looking after; we just did the playing bit.

I did actually like the idea once I'd got over my initial reservations, so I visited a local animal rescue centre to have a look, not really believing for one moment that I would actually end up having a furry friend of my own. In one cage were two young puppies who were adorable. One of them came to the front of the enclosure and made a fuss of me, and that was it. I decided he was the one for me.

All the checks were done; the garden was secure, and I was deemed to be a good potential "mother". I went back to the enclosure for one last look before signing the paperwork. This time the little girl dog came slowly forwards, sat down in front of me and gave me a look that seemed to say: "you're choosing me, not him". She stole my heart in that moment, and yet again, I followed my instinct and took another leap of faith and changed my mind. But did I choose her, or had she chosen me?

Rescue Dogs

Rescue dogs are heaven-sent, yes they're sent from
heaven above
To rescue us poor humans and to shower us with
love.
I certainly know that mine was my very own
superhero
She came into my life and lifted me up from well
below zero.
I had decided on her brother but went back for one
last look
She came to the front of the cage and started a new
chapter in my book.
Dogs love unconditionally, but I think rescue dogs
give more
Because on some level they understand that you
rescued them for sure!
So, they want to show you gratitude and lick you
from head to toe
To be your forever friend and protect you from all
types of foe.

But I want you to think deeply about who is really
rescuing who
Because rescue dogs are heaven-sent and there's a
reason yours chose you!

_____

To me, Pip was not just a rescue dog. She was
my companion, my angel, my furry friend, my
fitness instructor, my confidante, my rescuer - my
saviour. She gave me unconditional love, and it
was a pleasure and a privilege to learn how to give
it back. She got me out of the house walking once
or twice every day. The fresh air gave me an
appetite, not just for food but for life. I now
wanted to go out. I had a reason to go out.
Learning how to look after Pip somehow invoked
in me a feeling of wanting to look after myself too.
There was probably some part of me that realised
that this little furry bundle of love and fun was
totally relying on me and I was now ready to take
up the responsibility of caregiver. I knew that if I
didn't look after myself, then she wouldn't be
looked after; another step forward on the self-love
path. It made me feel good to be needed again.
She gave me a new purpose and a reason for being.

Pip became a new de-stressor. On a conscious level, I didn't realise this was happening, but as we walked together so often in the peace, silence and tranquillity of our local woods, I became more relaxed. The air was so fresh and infused with the smell of pine needles and sap. We explored off the beaten track, and I always felt safe with her little paws padding alongside me. When we left the main paths and went deeper into the forest, it felt like a cocoon, and the beautiful green mosses deadened any other sounds. The silence was intermittently broken only by my own feet snapping a twig underfoot.

I felt at one with nature, and it was during one of these "off the main path" walks that I came across a tree that looked like an elephant with two notches for eyes and dipped grooves down the side of the main trunk, making a column in the shape of the elephant's trunk. The rough bark resembled an elephant's tough looking skin. I felt drawn to hugging it. I could feel bark under my hands and face, but beneath that, I felt a deep peace. As we climbed higher after my "tree hug", I found a bench in a clearing, seemingly in the middle of nowhere, with no views other than trees. The "elephant tree" and the "lost bench" became my meditation spaces.

At this time, I had no idea that this was what I was doing. All I knew was that I was feeling wonderful after hugging a tree, and as there was never a soul around, I never felt self-conscious or stupid. I also used to sit for ages on the "lost bench." It was a real suntrap in the afternoons, and in the solitude and sunshine, I allowed my mind to drift. I had started "shinrin-yoku" (Japanese for forest bathing) and meditating, although I didn't realise this was what I had been doing. This is a poem I wrote back then that reflected my newfound inner peace.

Inside Out or Outside In

Outside is hustle and bustle
Inside is quiet and still
Outside, time goes so quickly
Inside, time stops at will.

Outside the world is revolving
Inside, it comes to a halt
Outside, a blaming society
Inside, no-one is at fault.

Outside, life runs so fast
Inside, it's slow and it's calm
Outside, there's hurt and there's hatred
Inside, where no-one can harm.

Outside, a life without living
Inside, fulfilment and love
Outside, disjointed and busy
Inside, connected to above.

Outside, where everyone worries
Inside, an oasis of peace
Outside, are negative feelings
Inside, all thoughts just cease.

Outside is where most of us look
Inside is all there can be
Outside, all doing, no being
Inside, where I find the real me.

Even though I was managing to function in life by now, a side effect of the depression for me (or maybe the numbing from the tablets) was that I had become quite forgetful, and my mind often felt full of fog. I had put on quite a bit of weight as I had been eating unhealthily.

The defining moment I realised something was really wrong was when I got into the car one day and placed my mobile phone, purse and car keys on the passenger seat. I went to turn on the ignition to realise that the keys weren't in my hand. I felt panic rise immediately. I even looked across at the front door to see if I had left the keys in the lock. Then the realisation quickly dawned that I had only just put the keys on the passenger seat literally a couple of seconds before. As I was flooded with both relief and embarrassment in equal measure, I realised that this was just another "stupid" thing I had found myself doing.

Other things included trying to move the mouse on my PC at work to discover that it was an apple I had in my hand! I had also left a colleague at work when only an hour previously, I had agreed to drop her off at her house on the way home. Another "mad moment" was leaving the motorway with two friends in the car to drop them off at their respective homes, but then going round the roundabout and driving straight back up onto the motorway with them still in the car!! I realised once more that I needed help.

By now, I was well ensconced in the holistic therapeutic world, so I booked a treatment with a Kinesiologist friend of mine who informed me I might have cerebral candida and suggested that giving up sugar and yeast would be beneficial. Not suddenly, but gradually. I thought this would be very difficult but that I would give it a go.

I followed her advice, and as a consequence, my mind fog did lift, and in addition to this, I had some other amazing side effects: my skin glowed, my eyes sparkled, my hair was glossy… and I dropped some weight. I felt as if someone had turned a light on inside my head and my body. I was sparkling, and I felt it, and this consequently boosted my confidence, my self-esteem and self-worth, which had all taken a battering. I had taken more steps towards self-love.

Feeling lighter and better than I had done in ages made me start to believe that perhaps I did have a future after all. Could I really be happy again?

From Singledom to Soulmate

As the years passed, I was starting to feel comfortable in my own skin, to be positive and optimistic. The benefits of singledom for me were little things like having the whole double bed to myself; not having to get up earlier as the bathroom was solely mine; being totally in charge of the TV remote control; not having to consult anyone about anything I wanted to do; eating what and when I wanted to – basically making decisions purely for me and for my needs.

It took time, but I started looking forward to getting up in the morning and going home to Pip every day. Looking back, I can see how I was living instinctively, spontaneously (when I could), getting fresh air, being out in nature, laughing with the dog, gazing in awe at starry skies and birds of prey, hugging trees, meditating, getting plenty of exercise, practising reiki and therapies and connecting with people again. I realised that I had choices, and my choices were actually a choice of attitude. I was still single, but I was no longer lonely.

I did join a social club for people who were single, but it wasn't a dating agency. I liked that. It was for people over 30 who happened to be on their own for whatever reason and to participate in various activities that could be difficult to enjoy on your own, such as go-carting, archery, badminton, cycling and much more.

I also reconnected with a former work colleague and we started to holiday together. She and I went to several Greek islands where I first experienced the phenomenon that is the "holiday romance", where I learnt that the only true part of that phrase is the word "holiday"! There wasn't a lot of romance, but it felt good to be the centre of attention for a short while. This time, though, I was more aware and could see the situation for exactly what it was. I thoroughly enjoyed myself and dated an older Greek guy, a much younger 18-year-old, a barman, a tour guide and all the while having lots of fun and laughter in the sun with my lovely friend.

I already had amazing support from health professionals, family and existing friends, but it was the support I had from new friends that was both surprising and especially heart-warming. I was lucky to connect with a gang of single girls who all worked at the same college satellite site. We were all in the same boat, so we gravitated together, and this resulted in more amazing holidays. I don't think I'd ever felt so free, and I found a new flirty side to myself. We had so much fun and laughter but yes, 'what goes on tour definitely stays on tour!'

Looking back, I probably should have done all this straight after leaving the polytechnic rather than settling down and getting married so soon, but then hindsight is a wonderful thing.

The many holiday dalliances actually made me start to think about whether I was becoming ready for a new relationship. I started to question what exactly I was looking for in a man, and one morning the following poem came to me…was I already practising the Law of Attraction? Was I putting my Cosmic Order in? Who knows?

Mr Right

Looking, seeking, searching out
To find that Mr Right
Good looking, honest and funny
To take me out at night.

Caring, kind and genuine too
Stocky, fit and tall
Strong, sporty and tactile
Oh yes, and that's not all!

He's got to have that spark,
That twinkle in his eye
That little mischievous look
Will make me pant and sigh!

Romantic, warm and generous
No little mummy's boy.
Preferably non-smoking
A cook will bring deep joy.

But does it matter in the end
'Cause if the spark is there
He could be very ancient
No teeth and not much hair!

Not looking and not searching
Just waiting for the sight
'Cause I'll know when I see him
My very own Mr Right!

I've since learnt that if you don't ask, you don't get, but if you do ask and don't attach any outcome or expectation AND it's for your highest good, then it will be delivered when the timing is right for you. So don't stop asking for what you want but let go of the outcome or expectation.

I was starting to feel good in my own skin. These non-pressure short-term relationships boosted my confidence. Interestingly, though, they also made me aware of how people want to label and pigeonhole others. *"What do you do?" "How old are you?" "Are you single/married?"* I was asked so many questions it felt as if they needed to get a handle on me and put me in some sort of specific bracket or box in their minds, and I realised that I didn't want to be pigeon-holed and I still don't. I don't like labels. This poem actually came to me out of the blue and made me start to realise that I was (and still am) a unique, special individual, as is everyone else.

DebS

Don't pigeonhole or label me
'Cause I am who I am
Not just a list of facts
And certainly not a sham.

'Cause I am different every day
Yet parts remain the same
A contradiction in terms
Living is the name of the game.

A game of two halves perhaps
One serious and one all fun
One that likes to slob on the settee
One that loves going for a run.

One that likes to read comics
But also likes hefty books.
One that likes to be presentable
But is not concerned how she looks.

One who is very caring and kind
But can be self-centred too.
There's loads more I could add
But I'll leave some work up to you.

I guess you still would like some clues
A hint of who I am?
So here's a list of facts
Did I say list? I did - oh damn!

_____

    I felt that I knew what I wanted in a fella, but they never really matched up, so I eventually allowed myself to be single. I don't suppose it was a conscious choice, I think I just gave up looking, and in the process, I really started to learn to love myself. I was thoroughly enjoying just being with the dog and having my own space, mistress of my own destiny (as much as any of us are). I didn't have to compromise my life or myself in any way or be careful about what I said, or walk on eggshells around someone else's feelings, or feel unsure of myself in a relationship, or take the time to get to know someone from scratch or worry about what I looked like first thing in the morning. I found a whole host of benefits to being single, and I really started to enjoy it just being me and my dog, who never worried about what I looked like or whether I snored (yes, apparently, I have snored since I was a child) or what I ate, or what I watched on TV or listened to on the radio or whether I got up early or went to bed late, or walked in the rain for hours, or cried myself to sleep, and she was always ready for cuddles whenever I wanted them. I felt unfettered and free.

It's amazing that as I understood myself more and received more self-awareness, I was living "in the flow", being spontaneous, accepting new challenges, connecting with people, having fun, meditating or sitting quietly, practising my therapies, learning about energies and more therapeutic interventions, I found that all this was freeing me up. From the dark depths of despair, I felt I was finally coming into the light.

Another "side effect" of all this enjoyment of life resulted in me eventually meeting my significant other. It happened after about five years of being truly single and when I wasn't actively looking anymore. In between, I had a couple of short-term relationships, and they were lovely and filled a gap, but I knew I hadn't found the right man yet. I wasn't really looking, so it wasn't important. It's interesting that when I surrendered to being empty and allowing myself to live in the flow of life, to accept life as it was, to relax into life, then things started happening.

For instance, when I was at the depths of despair and was empty and felt I had nothing left to give, I surrendered. I was full of anxiety, stress and angst, and somehow, I was managing to live day to day but from a place of hopelessness and darkness, a place I felt I had been forced into by circumstances beyond my control. Even though I felt I was in a negative position of having "no choice", when I was at my emptiest and surrendered, things started to change.

Perversely, I was now living in a similar vein, still "empty", but it was from a completely different perspective of "choice", where I felt I did have options; I did have something to give, and even though I didn't know where to give it, I wasn't worrying about it, and I was indeed giving it to myself without really knowing it. I was still living day-to-day, but this time from a place of positivity, optimism, hope, joy, a lighter place and as a consequence, more synchronicities were occurring.

An example of these synchronicities is that jobs seemed to come to me over the years. One instance was when I was teaching in the community for a local college. I was blessed to have a succession of part-time jobs to cover the summer period when those classes weren't running. Again, they just appeared in my life. What's so interesting is that I had no expectations of these jobs appearing, nor getting them. I wasn't even looking, and each time a job or contract finished, another appeared to take its place. Life was sending me an abundance of opportunities, and I was taking them without hesitation. I now know that I was saying "yes" to the Universe.

The next synchronicity is one of the most serendipitous of them all. I continued with my therapeutic qualifications and was studying for a Clinical Hypnotherapy diploma. At the time, I was an NVQ (National Vocational Qualification) assessor, and while I was waiting for one of my candidates, I picked up the local newspaper to browse through when an advert caught my eye from the charity MIND. They were looking for volunteer therapists to work with them. I ripped it out and put it in my pocket to keep, thinking that I would like to do that once I had completed my hypnotherapy course and had a bit more experience.

I was driving home when my phone buzzed with a notification of a voicemail. It was from a friend informing me that there was a job that was "perfect for me" in the local paper, as a therapist for a children's charity close to where I lived. I hadn't seen the advert. Surely, I would have noticed it? I stopped to buy the paper and looked through it. I saw the advert for MIND and turned the page. The advert for the charity was directly on the back of that particular page. I pulled the ripped-out piece of paper from my pocket, and sure enough, the ad for the therapist's job was on the back of the one for the volunteers for MIND. This blew my "mind", I can tell you.

I applied and got the job, and when one contract ended, another job appeared. Life continued in the same vein until my last employed job, when we were all suddenly and unexpectedly made redundant. It was a very difficult time because we were told to attend the office at the end of that day and were informed that the company was no longer solvent and to get our things and leave, just like that. It was a surprise, a huge shock, a life-changing bolt out of the blue. But by this time, I was a completely different person from when I suffered such a huge shock previously. This time I had energy therapies to fall back on, to use to process the emotions.

I was, thankfully by now, an optimist with an undercurrent of hope and positivity running through me all the time. I remember beneath the initial negative emotions, feeling that this could be one of the best things that could have happened, but I didn't know why. I felt a sense of freedom descend, and sure enough, I was right. It did turn out to be one of the best things that could have happened. I am so grateful that again, out of a negative event, a positive outcome occurred. The Universe guided me from one job to another for many years, each being provided with divine timing. I trusted and went with the flow and took a leap of faith each time, and it always worked out.

The other thing that happened is that I met a man… twice! Yes, it was the same man. Another bit of synchronicity. Cast your mind back to the time when I had joined a social club. They organised a separate activity for one of the sports I had loved from school and in polytechnic but had not played since then: badminton. So, I decided to pick up my racket again and joined their club. I didn't know a soul who was playing, and it was actually a difficult thing for me to do, to walk in on my own. But I girded my loins, put my big girl's pants on, decided that the outcome would be worth the discomfort and I went along one night.

There was a chap on the court with his back to me, and I remember thinking that I liked the look of his legs. I quite liked the look of his face, too, when he turned around, but I instantly dismissed this thought as I wasn't looking for a relationship anymore. The players used to go out for a drink afterwards, again not my thing really, but I went so as not to appear stand-offish. With all my newfound confidence, I started flirting a little and chatting him up, using my new chat-up line of "being a masseuse". He told awful jokes and asked me whether I could cook, which put me off a bit, but I somehow found myself giving him my business card anyway. I went to the club a couple of times, but as the standard of play wasn't what I had been used to, I stopped going.

Here comes more synchronicity - if you can take any more? I was still doing some of the other activities with my new single girlfriends and making new friends at work. One of these ladies had also gone through a divorce, and we were all supporting her through it. One day she told me she felt ready to start socialising again, so I suggested taking her to the social club where she could meet people, join in some of the activities and just get out and about as I had done.

(One vital piece of information that you need to know before I continue with this bit of the story is that I had put a few of my poems together in a little booklet to sell for charity.) I told my friend that I would take her to the social evening to introduce her to a few people I knew, and I also decided to take some of my poetry booklets to sell. What a surprise it was to see the guy from the badminton club there. I later discovered that he had also taken his friend who had recently split up from a relationship to introduce him to people he knew. Neither of us ever went to the social side usually, so what were the chances of us both being there on the same day, at the same time?

Anyway, we got talking, and he asked me whether I was still going to the social badminton club. I said I hadn't been in ages because the standard wasn't really high enough to have any decent games. He divulged that he had stopped going for similar reasons. On the spur of the moment, he invited me and my friend along to another club he belonged to, which met the following night. Curiosity must have got the better of him because he then asked me what I had in my hand, so I explained about my poems and that I was selling them for charity, and he kindly bought one.

The following night my friend and I turned up at the other club because we really did want to play some good badminton. I thoroughly enjoyed myself and had no further designs on this man until he told me that he had stopped by a beach that day to have his lunch and decided to read some of my poems. He then had the temerity to ask whether I had actually written them myself. I told him he was a cheeky git, and of course, I had. He then said something that almost floored me. He said that one of them had made him cry. I may well have been doing an impersonation of a fish at that point. I didn't know what to say, but his admitting this made me see him in a completely different light to how I had previously. Him admitting his vulnerability and showing a sensitive side was a turning point.

Over time we became friends, and I discovered that the person I had met initially was just covering over the real person within. Gradually our friendship deepened, we laughed together a lot, found out we had similar values, morals and interests, and as we spent more and more time together, we discovered how compatible we were and became closer and closer. One night after having been for a post-badminton drink, we stood opposite each other in the rain, neither of us showing signs of wanting to leave. He hadn't got a coat, and I was wearing an old Parka, big enough for two, so I opened the coat to shelter him from the rain. He stepped in, put his arms around me and kissed me. I melted and in that moment, realised that I had fallen in love with this man.

When I eventually allowed myself to fully trust him (which took a while, not through any fault of his, just because of my past experience getting in the way); I realised I had found a safe pair of hands, an even keel, a safe haven, a rock and a deep, contented love. He also understood what it was like to go through a divorce as he had been through the process himself. He later let slip that he had stopped attending the social badminton club because I had stopped going, and he had kept my business card in the car all that time; so had he been practising the Law of Attraction too?

And again, was it synchronicity, fate, Law of Attraction that progressed the relationship? The same friend who told me about the therapist job in the paper knew I was looking for ways to make a bit of extra money. So, she suggested I rent my house out for a week as there was a national event that was happening locally, where she knew they were crying out for accommodation. I told her I couldn't do it because I didn't have anywhere to go. Her answer was to move in with my boyfriend for the week. Bearing in mind it was both me and my dog, and he came from a family who had never had pets, I thought it was a big ask. But as I had become a believer in the "if you don't ask, you don't get" philosophy, I asked, and he said yes. So both myself and my dog decamped for a week. What came next was really unexpected. At the end of the week, when it was time for me to move back home, he asked whether I had to go and invited me and my dog to stay.

Well, I wasn't expecting that but stay I did. We both said yes to the Universe and it has worked so far.

There is a saying: "ask and it shall be given", and I now believe that if you are truly ready for it, then it is given, so what else would I be gifted with?

Dearth and Death

The interesting thing is that during the time I was with my partner (I like to call it my "contented period"), my poetry slowed down to a trickle as my life stabilised. I was still spending plenty of time out in nature with the dog. I joined a spiritual/meditation group and started doing yoga. I was happy in my workplaces, using my therapies, had a loving, cheerful partner and a dog who loved me unconditionally. I was truly content with my life.

Alongside this contentment, almost as if I no longer needed to have an emotional outlet because I had found new ones, my outpourings of rhyme faded away. I didn't stop the poems; they just stopped coming. I occasionally made up a few for friends' birthdays and Mother's Day, but the deep, heartfelt, ready-made poems stopped coming.

From the time I started dating my partner, I only produced two poems, which when I was used to being so prolific was a bit of a surprise, but I thought of it as something that used to happen in that previous chapter of my life. This one was quite deep and spiritual/philosophical, which came as I was exploring my own spirituality and life philosophies.

_____

All That We Are

For all that we are…..we are nothing.
For all that we are…..we are all.
For all that we are…..we are human.
For all that we are…..we stand tall.

You are nothing…..yet you inhabit this planet.
You are all…..and have been since your birth.
You are human….. and you make this world great.
You stand tall…..you're unique on this earth!

_____

The other was almost a request to the Universe, a cosmic request if you like, for what I wanted out of my relationship in order for me to feel that I was loved.

Expressions of Love

A present bought
A kindly thought
A word from the heart
Mending a part
A smile on the face
Being in the right place
A meal cooked by you
A day at the zoo
That special look
A very good book
Planning a treat
A break in the heat
A lovely soft kiss
A statement of bliss
A favour for free
Planting a tree
A reliable car
Naming a star
Telling a joke
Hearing words spoke
Mowing the lawn
Not pouring scorn

A trip on a plane
A walk in the rain
Tickets for a show
Flowers to grow
Picnic in the park
Fireworks after dark
Time with no haste
An arm around the waist
Breakfast in bed
Massage on the head
An offer of aid
A bill secretly paid
Sharing the load
Not trying to goad
Special music recorded
Expensive item afforded
Listening to woes
Protection from foes
Chocolate or sweets
Rubbing the feet
Talking of fears
Wiping the tears

Putting out the bin   A bottle of good wine
A big silly grin   The surprise of a lifetime

The smallest of things, can satisfy dreams
A word or an act has so much impact
Remember to treat and keep your love sweet.

Just do as you would be done to
And prove the words "I love you!"

Life was "hunky-dory" and bubbled along nicely until mid-2015 when my gorgeous dog, Pip, became ill. She was getting old and grey around the muzzle anyway. She was still eating and wanting to go out for walks, but her back legs weren't as strong, and I felt like I could see her almost visibly shrinking each day. I thought perhaps she had arthritis as she had been starting to struggle going up and down the stairs. So, I took her to the vets who suggested blood tests and unfortunately, I was given the sad news that her kidneys were packing in, and she didn't have long to live. The vet suggested I book her in for "the injection" for the following day as her kidney function was so low. In shock, I panicked and asked the vet if there was anything that could be done to help her be more comfortable. She suggested that I could take Pip to the local PDSA about 20 minutes away, where they would keep her comfortable overnight and administer drugs.

My brain had gone into stress response, and all the blood had flooded to the back of my head where you then cannot make any rational decision. I immediately agreed because all I could think about was that she would be comfortable and not in any pain, but as I was driving down the motorway, I suddenly realised what I was actually doing. I was going to leave my beloved companion of 15 years with strangers overnight on what would be the last night she would have on planet earth. So, I pulled into a lay-by and rang the vet back to tell her I'd changed my mind and I would take Pip home with me before bringing her in the following day.

As it happened, we had to pass where she and I used to live and had five years together on our own before moving in with my partner, and I had what I thought was the fanciful thought of just showing her the woods again where we used to go walking for old times' sake. Stupid really.

I parked up, and to my delight and astonishment, she jumped out of the car like a puppy, walked ahead while I was locking the car, and she turned and looked at me as if saying, "well, come on then". It was like having my healthy girl back again. As always, we walked together in companionable silence. The woods hadn't changed; they still smelt of pine needles and sap. This time we stayed on the main path, where the sound of her claws tapping on the gravel echoed inside my head. My mind felt empty of everything other than the devastating knowledge that this would be the last time we would ever walk here. The greyness of the sky reflected my feelings of sadness inside. It started to drizzle, the cold on my skin matching the coldness I felt in my heart. As we had stopped on a whim, I didn't have a coat. I called her to go back to the car, but she just kept on walking as if she had all the energy in the world. So, we walked until I could no longer see, as the rain trickled down my face, mixing with my tears as the realisation that there would be no more walks in the woods.

(I feel I must mention here that The Eagles, one of my favourite bands, released a new album in 2007 called "Long Road Out of Eden", on which is an acapella song called "No More Walks in the Wood". I felt it had been written for me and Pip; the words and the haunting sound of their voices and stunning harmonies struck me in my heart when I first heard it, and it brought me to tears. It broke me every time I heard it. However, since using energy techniques, I have managed to release many of the connected emotions to the grief I was experiencing at the time; I can now hear it and sing along and just appreciate the sheer beauty of it.)

A very strange thing happened later after we got home. Pip went out into the garden for a wee, but she disappeared. I went to check on her, and I couldn't see her anywhere. My heart jumped into my mouth. The garden is completely enclosed, so I knew she couldn't get out. I fully expected to find her curled up somewhere, having passed away. Bizarrely she was behind the shed, somewhere she had never been before, to my knowledge. I said to my partner that I thought she was trying to hide from us and perhaps pass away without us seeing it happen. A fanciful thought that perhaps she was trying to spare us some heartache?

That night she was allowed to sleep on the bed. I wrapped myself around her and gave her Reiki all night as I know it can help people who are ready to pass over to go in peace. The following morning, I fully expected to find her gone, but no, she was still with us. We were up early as we hadn't had much sleep. It was a beautiful sunny day, so I carried her in her bed and laid her on the patio outside in the sun because, like me, she loved the sun. When she was a puppy, she sneaked up to lie in the sun on my sunbed the minute I had vacated it to go and get a drink. It made me laugh then, and this image still makes me laugh as it brings back that happy memory.

I went back inside to make a cup of tea while my partner was getting dressed and when I went back out, her bed was empty. Again, she had disappeared, but this time she wasn't behind the shed. She didn't come when I called her, and I had the crazy thought that the angels had come down and taken her. I shouted for my partner to come and help me look because I really panicked.

This time, though, she had gone down behind the back of the decking, again, somewhere she had never been before. I truly felt she was telling us that she was ready to go and that she was trying to find somewhere that she could just lie down and leave in peace. This was a tricky one for me. Should I cancel the appointment with the vet and just let nature take its course and let Pip do whatever it was she was trying to do?

I sat with her, willing her to give me a message, to put some words into my head, to let me know what she needed, but I heard nothing. So, we took her to the vet, and I held her, silently thanking her for her love and her companionship while she was put to sleep. It was such a peaceful process, and even though my heart was in bits, my partner and I were both in tears; I knew deep down inside it was the right thing to do. I wouldn't have wanted to see her suffer or be in pain.

Yet again, a huge part of my life had gone, just like that. It created another huge void, just like the last time. A light in my life had been extinguished, and once more, I was broken. This time, though, it was different. The hurt was still as intense; the sharp, piercing pain in the heart, the deep ache in the gut, the rivers of tears were still the same, but this time I was different. This time I had now learnt so much about gratitude, positivity, hope, optimism, joy, living for the now, love, and she had taught me so much about these. I do remember saying many times that I have since tried to live like my dog: happy, playful, eating, drinking water, sleeping soundly, stretching, cuddling often, loving unconditionally, walking daily, accepting life for what it was and just being present in every moment.

Even though I was again going through a bereavement, this time I had tools, therapies, interventions - call them what you will - to get me through. And I had gratitude. Despite the tears and the sadness, I was aware of the river of optimism and hope running through me. I would tell people who knew she had gone that I was lucky to have had her for so long and how much she had taught me. I believe this also helped get me through. In addition, I had discovered Seratone 5HTP, which is a natural precursor to Serotonin which can get affected during the stress of a traumatic event. It's something I keep in my medicine cabinet to this day to take if I feel myself dipping. So far, I've only needed to take it once again when Dad died.

So, I started taking care of myself even more. I practised daily gratitude, I was still doing yoga and meditation, and my partner was wonderfully supportive of me during this time which was a huge help. I saw the silver linings in all the black clouds. I started being more thankful for having less commitment and more time to do other things.

The one thing I did struggle with for years was going out for a walk on my own - without her. It didn't feel right. I felt like I was being disloyal. Silly, really, but the feeling was there, and it felt real to me.

We often dismiss our own or others' feelings as silly or not important, and others do it to us too, but if those feelings feel real to the individual, then they are important and shouldn't be dismissed. Even though they are just energy and can be shifted, they matter in the moment and should be acknowledged, accepted and allowed to go.

The first time I tried to go out for a walk on my own, I almost had a panic attack. I pushed through though and went out but felt so lost without my gorgeous dog on the end of a lead, I couldn't face doing it again for quite some time. I was fine walking with someone else, but it had been something she and I did together. This seemingly silly idea has taken some work to release. It always amazes me how many issues, beliefs and thought patterns we cling to to keep our world feeling safe.

It has taken writing this book to make me realise that this is something I hadn't chosen to look at in-depth until I was ready.

I would say it took me quite some time to finish grieving properly, and yet when I wrote this part of the book, tears flooded my face, and I sobbed again. I thought then that perhaps grief never truly goes. Although the optimistic part of me knows now that this is just a negative belief. I realised that these emotions were stored somewhere, hidden away somewhere inside me, so I decided to stop doing therapies on anyone else and to focus solely on me. I chose to work on myself and the trapped emotions caused by the traumatic events in my life, no matter how big or small right up to this point. I chose to clear many of the emotions that had come up in the process of writing this book.

During this time, I learnt additional techniques such as Access Conscious, EAM (Energy Alignment Method), and Divine Energy Healing. I have acquired a Healy frequency machine and am training to be a Healy Coach, and I qualified as an Akashic Records Consultant. I already had EFT (Emotional Freedom Technique) and Modern Energy self-help tools in my toolbox to add to all the therapies I had learnt to help other people, such as hypnotherapy, reiki, dowsing, vibrational medicine, etc. I have been an avid student of all things energy and holistic. EAM was pivotal most of all in releasing most of my issues, with Akashic Records being the icing on the cake.

NB: During the re-edits in 2021, I now have moist eyes when I read this, but no pain in my heart, only gratitude. Thanks to EAM, I have progressed. After releasing those heavy intense emotions following that emotional breakdown when I wrote about Pip in this story, I unexpectedly received my first poem download again.

This poem brought in a whole new set of thoughts for me to dive into; an investigation of the numerous roles she played in my life, which then led me to look at the concept of all the roles I previously expected my significant others to play.

My Constant Companion

My constant companion has now left my side
My shadow no longer is seen
Apart from the shadow cast deep in my heart
Like no other love ever been.

My constant companion has gone to the skies
The space left; a huge gaping hole
No more barks at the post nor wags of the tail
Like the heart is ripped out of my soul.

My constant companion is still in my mind
A rescue dog that rescued me back
An angel from above that came down to earth
For the sake of a crisp little snack.

My constant companion was only on loan
A fact that I now know for certain
'Cause she's gone back to the angels high in the sky
Looking down at me through the cloud curtain.

My constant companion has taught me so much
That life is not all that complex
Just eat, drink and walk, sleep, play and hug
Show love and have a good stretch!

My constant companion gave me so much love
Regardless of mood, stress or strain
Consistently constantly there by my side
In the sun, wind, snow and the rain.

My constant companion has left me enlightened
With realisation that things are not ours
No permanency here, all borrowed - not had
The universe lends for so many hours.

My constant companion, though her body's not here
Her soft fur no longer to touch
Her love is wedged so deep in my heart
Her spirit will guide me so much.

My constant companion has now found her peace
No more pain nor suffering to endure
I'll always be grateful to my gorgeous girl Pip
Unconditional love she taught me for sure.

Some of you who are pet owners may identify with this. My dog was my surrogate child, my guardian angel, my saviour from depression, my fitness guru, my companion, my sounding board, my comedian, and much more. She gave me unconditional love and for seemingly little reward. All she needed was cuddles, regular walks, food, a comfy bed, water and play. That was it. It made me wonder whether perhaps that's all we really need? It made me inspect my idea of what love is and my relationship in my marriage. Most people love conditionally; they will love you if you love them in a certain way, give them a certain thing or behave in a certain way. Most of us are guilty of this. It seems very difficult for human beings to love unconditionally without criticism or judgement or wanting or needing something in return for giving love.

Another thing I realised from the roles my dog played in my life woke me up to the fact that I put a lot of expectations on other people being responsible for my happiness and had probably done so all my life. This was a real wake-up call. It was a definite lightbulb moment. In retrospection, I realised that I had expected my ex-husband to be my best friend, my fitness companion, my girlfriend, my husband, my comedian, my confidante, my everything. (At this moment, a Barry White track has popped into my head. "My first, my last, my everything".) Could this be where it all went wrong? Had I expected too much from him? I will never know. I did know that I could not go down that rocky road of wanting to know "why" all over again. So I chose to let this go.

Pip leaving such a big hole in my life made me realise I had to change, and the only one who could make that happen was me. Not having her presence left a huge gap which gave me space and a platform to really start studying myself, to really look at myself in the mirror and get to know the true me. And as that wonderful Michael Jackson song "Man in the Mirror" says: *"I'm starting with the (wo)man in the mirror; I'm asking (her) him to change his ways…take a look at yourself and make the change".*

Once the intense grief stage diminished, I decided that my new goals needed to be to learn to live like my dog, to love life, to live in the flow and in each and every present moment and to learn to love unconditionally. I think it's what we all should be aiming for. Forget the material goals of a nice house, car, holidays abroad, lovely clothes etc. Yes, all these are wonderful to have if you are lucky enough to have them. But surely, the most important thing is how we are as people? To honour, respect, be grateful, kind, caring, thoughtful, compassionate, tolerant, non-judgemental, to live life to its fullest and to love life, other people and ourselves surely is the greatest gift we can have?

This would lead me very nicely into the next chapter of my life story, as this was a major part of my path to "delightenment". However, there were further traumas to come, which have all continued to open up my mind, reignite my poetry and allowed me to realise how far I have come since that suicidal thought, the depression as a result of the trauma of my divorce and my inability to handle what that massive change wrought.

It had been two years without my lovely dog before the poems started to arrive again. From the time of writing "My Constant Companion" in

2017, slowly, they started to appear again. Initially, it was a small trickle until the end of 2018, when that trickle became a deluge.

Poetry Diarrhoea

When someone has something to say
They usually speak it in words
I suppose some may write it down as a song
For pop stars to sing – not for the birds!

But for me this so does not happen
Mine are all coming out in rhyme
And lately, just like diarrhoea
It's happening all of the time!

I'm not sure what's happening to me
Is this a blessing or is this a curse?
To be waking up every morning
With all of this rhyming verse.

And it's disrupting my usual sleep patterns
So tired now – I'm starting to be
This week in the early hours of the morning
Each dawn I've been able to see.

The moment my brain comes awake
In the early wee hours of the morn
A spark of an idea, just a couple of lines
And then suddenly a poem in full form.

My brain, it appears, is overloaded
Words into verses they just keep on coming
And I have to get up and write them all down
'Til my fingers and hands they are numbing!

I'm curious as to where they come from
I'm pleased but at the same time I'm not
It feels like they come straight through to my pen
Is it a talent or is it really all rot?

I don't know if they're suddenly going to stop
Like they did back many years ago
Maybe they will or maybe they won't
At this point I really don't know.

So for now, I must make the most of my time
With this condition of poetry diarrhoea
As long as the words come from my head to my pen
And they don't start coming out of my rear!

―――――――――――――――――――――――

What I also noticed was that some of the poems arrived in a different style, which was both surprising and appealing. And subsequently, even though the majority reverted to the same rhythm and rhyme as my previous style, the subject matter was much more varied. They were wide-ranging, thought-provoking, philosophical, funny, heart-warming and I poked fun at myself, which was so different to how they had arrived when they started. There was one about Christmas, New Year, the different masks that women wear, dementia, NHS Heroes, a car salesman, menopause, wishing upon a star, hedgehogs, starlings, love, grief, mourning, grey hair and one was even set to music in my head. It's unfinished but was set to the Peter Sarstedt song "Where do you go to my lovely?". I adapted the lyrics to talk about where a dementia sufferer goes to in their head. The poems just kept coming.

One of the "different style" poems was brought on by a series of difficult life events. So many things were happening, seemingly all at once: Dad having a cancer op, seeing our friend damage his ankle while we were playing badminton, having my partner's parents in separate respite homes in different towns, his mum with a broken arm, his dad also diagnosed with dementia, my Mum was due to have cataract ops and was diagnosed with heart problems as well as her IBS playing up - all this was just before Christmas 2018; in fact, all within the space of just 14 days.

Just 14 Days

Broken ankle must rankle;
Torn ligs, no more jigs;
Poor friend, soon will mend.
Heart and eyes, ahead lies;
Bad tummy, poorly Mummy.
Cancer scare, skin tear;
Had op, scar on top;
Stitches out, Dad didn't shout.
Broken bone, care home;

Parents apart, breaks our hearts;
No longer a pair, dementia care;
Where to go, we didn't know,
Social care, let's be fair,
Amazing peeps. Now they can sleep.
Futures saved, decisions made;
Places found, safe and sound.
Emotions waver, hope's our saviour!

I had also been going through the menopause
and that seemed to rear its ugly head too - a fact
which I put down to additional stress. Stress
hormones definitely made my menopause worse,
which is another reason for making sure I stay as
stress-free as possible.

I wrote the following poem after a particularly
bad spell.

Menopause and Mojo

Oh no mojo, not again! Where have you gone?
One minute you're here with me, the next you've
moved along.

The mood swings come, both up and down
One minute there's a smile and the next there's a
frown.
The slightest things affect me; so sensitive I can be
Crying at a silly film or someone felling a tree!
My coping mechanisms have diminished at such a
rapid pace
Organisational skills gone up the spout, so I'm now
not on the case.
My body temperature gauge has really thrown a
wobbly
Hot flushes, night sweats abound and my skin's gone
kind of knobbly!
My sleep patterns are hugely disturbed and that's just
another thing
From sleeping like a baby or a log to then hearing
everything.
Eating like the proverbial pig. Yes, that's everything
in sight
No diets or dry months work; forget any food that's
light!
Our body shape transitions; an extra stomach now
appears
And I'm really not going to comment on our thighs,
hips and rears!
Yet still we seem to manage, to push right on
through life

Even though inside we scream and want to stab
someone with a knife!
I also feel sorry for our men who can never
understand
For they can't know what we're going through; to
them it's a foreign land.
With all these things we have, we women are still so
strong
Periods, babies and menopause; the list is terribly
long.
And yet in other countries, their women don't get the
same
So is it beliefs and programming, or is sugar really to
blame?
Perhaps if we eat real clean and walk 10,000 steps a
day
And meditate each morning, then health will come
our way?
But if we don't have mojo to get back on this path
Then back to square one we go; life really is having a
laugh!
So mojo, I ask, where have you gone? I really need
you back
Without you I have to start again, without you there
is a lack.
Mojo, I beg of you, return, come back right now
You're so important to me, to stop me being a cow.

Mojo, I'm sorry, please forgive me, without you I feel blue
I appreciate you, oh so much, thank you and I love you.

What this highlighted for me was that I was feeding my menopause. I was giving it attention and focus. I was constantly talking about the sweats, the foggy brain, the lack of organisation, the additional belly fat, the decrease in energy, the disrupted sleep patterns. I was allowing it to take over my life and become my whole focus and the sole topic of conversation. By doing this, I was actually making it worse, so I experimented by not talking about them, by giving them gratitude and love, and slowly, gradually, the symptoms subsided.

I also discovered Serenity hormone cream, which definitely helped some of the symptoms. I'm still working on the belly fat though!

Another life-changing episode was also happening alongside the menopause. Over time Dad's health was steadily deteriorating, and our first major challenge was when he could no longer walk around himself, and we had to take him out in a wheelchair. Dad had suffered from sleep apnoea and aneurysms for years; then, he was diagnosed with heart disease, and there was a gradual deterioration towards dementia and cancer. Luckily, he was one of the happier dementia sufferers, and he didn't seem to notice the cancer, thank goodness. He was still pretty jolly and cheerful in himself and had retained his sense of humour, but he was becoming less engaged, more forgetful, quieter and as Mum put it: "not the man she knew and loved". Over the space of two years until his death in June 2019, we slowly started to lose him, a little bit at a time. Each time I visited, I could see a deterioration. It was a difficult period because there was absolutely nothing anyone could do other than make him feel as comfortable and loved as possible. We all knew that he was slowly moving closer to his end of life, but none of us knew (as none of us do) when this would actually be.

I wanted to help and did as much as I could to support them both during this time but felt helpless on the whole. One of the things I did, though, was to write a poem for him to try and help him with his failing memory. It was based on my memories of him as I was growing up. I'm so glad I wrote this because it was a perfect tribute for me to read out at the celebration of his life after his internment.

One day, around the time he had pretty much stopped going out at all, I had gone to visit. He suddenly stood up (with difficulty) and said he wanted to go out. I was initially taken aback; he hadn't wanted to go out for some time, but something inside me kicked in. Instinct perhaps? I knew on some level that it was the right thing to do, however difficult it might be to achieve. So I didn't hesitate and said: "OK Dad, where do you want to go?" "I don't know," he said, "I just want to go out." So, I decided to take him out. I had no plan formulated. I just wanted to do this for him.

It was spontaneous and turned out to be a wonderful gift for me to be able to give him. Mum was initially against it and didn't want me to take him out, but I said we were going, and in the end, she came with us too. We managed to get him into the car, albeit very slowly, and I decided to drive up the mountain road where I recalled there being a lay-by near a stud farm. I parked up, and we asked Dad if he wanted to get out to stroke the horses, but he didn't, which was a shame.

It was a beautiful day, the sky being a perfect cerulean blue with big marshmallow clouds casting shadows over the green surface of the Black Mountains. Even though the air was fresh and crisp, the sunshine warmed our skin as Mum and I stroked the long necks of the horses. They snuffled and sniffed our hands, clearly disappointed that we hadn't brought any mints or carrots. Whether it was the warmth of the sun or the effect of the fresh air, Dad eventually drifted off to sleep, and we took him home. It is a precious memory, and I feel glad that I did that for him. I'm not sure he left the house again after that, other than for hospital appointments.

It was tough seeing Dad diminish and become a frightened old man. It was equally tough seeing Mum running herself ragged looking after him and always putting him first. Yet it was also a beautiful time because what I saw in this was their love for each other and Mum's selfless giving to the man she loved. I admire my mum for her determination to do everything she could to care for Dad at home until his death. I'm inspired by her ability to just keep going, take each day at a time, and she continues to do so. I loved my dad for the cheerful, light-hearted soul that he was, and I love and am proud of my mum for being the amazing strong woman she is. I wrote this poem inspired by their deep abiding love for each other.

_____

A Love That Lasts

A love that lasts is a beautiful thing, that's lovely to behold
It is a true love story that's just waiting to be told.
It's about two people who are in love; who make it to the end
Despite what life throws at them and drives them round the bend.
Weather is so fickle and life can be just like this
We know bad weather ends and the sunshine brings such bliss.

The laughter is like rainbows that light up the sky so bright
It's similar to the last kiss you have before sleeping late at night.
What is it that makes love endure between two human beings?
It's a secret we may never learn, but it's fab when we find those feelings.
Some of us can only wonder at how lengthy relationships last.
For we may never get there, but we'll try – and have a blast!
It's all about small moments; holding hands; looking into the eyes
Right at each other's souls; reflecting depths like the starry skies.
A love that lasts is a lovely thing, and it's beautiful to behold
It is really a true love story that perhaps can never be told.

––––––––––––––––––––––––––––

The grief I felt after Dad died was full of conflict. I was, on the one hand, relieved that he was no longer suffering and that Mum could rest, recuperate and was no longer living with the daily stress of caring for him; yet, on the other hand, Dad was gone, and I know Mum would have had him back like a shot. This poem reflects the conflict I felt.

Sadness and Gladness

Why is it my mourning comes out early in the morning
The sadness breaks into me just as the day is dawning.
But it's not the mourning of the person who so recently left
It's for the person they were before that makes me feel bereft.
Sadness and gladness, they obviously go hand in hand
Like the angel and the devil, the oceans and the land.
The sadness for the Dad we knew that makes tears pour like rain
But also gladness that he's gone and no longer in any pain.
This conflict of emotions can pull me in opposite ways
They seem to go together, though, like two parts of a Shakespeare play.

Sadness for the Dad we knew when on his own, he
could walk
The gladness because at the very end, he could barely
talk.
The gladness that for Mum now, the caring
pressure's eased
The sadness that he's not there, for us all to tease.
Six weeks on, reality kicks in – things can never be
the same
So I'll let the sadness go, 'cause the gladness keeps
me sane.
I'll let the tears pour down my face because I miss
my smiley Dad
The laughing, joking, happy one 'cause those
memories make me glad.

I understood and accepted that Dad had a
good life; it was something he always used to say.
So, despite the sadness and upset of him passing
away, for me, it felt easier (not sure that's the right
word) to deal with. Or maybe it was that I had
now had three bereavements in my life, so was I
getting more adept at dealing with them?

All I know is that I dealt with Dad's death much better than the bereavement of my divorce and the bereavement from my dog. Each time I reinforced resilience, and I am certain that without EFT (Emotional Freedom Technique also known as Tapping) in the earlier period after Pip passed away and subsequently learning the therapeutic power of EAM, which helped me get through the last few years, I would not have progressed in such a positive way. I'm not saying I haven't grieved; I have cried buckets, but I have come through it with a sense of underlying calm, optimism and hope, which I didn't have the first time around.

Each time it was different. This time using energy therapies and through my poems, I was able to express and release the myriad of feelings and emotions surrounding grief and bereavement in addition to writing about things I was grateful for, such as the NHS Heroes and St David's Hospice (the cancer charity that was so supportive of Mum). I found myself writing about important topics such as the homeless, where I tried to put myself in their shoes, plastics, climate change and more ordinary things like cloud watching, plants and space and even what someone had for their breakfast on holiday!

Broccoli for Breakfast

When I go on holiday, I like to see a host of brand new sights
I love observing people all day and right through into the night.
And just when I think I've seen it all – something new surprises me.
A plate of broccoli for breakfast when I thought it was only for tea!
And sharing the plate were carrots; small, orange and round
A partial rainbow contrast against the green of his broccoli mound.
Even the waiting staff seemed perplexed by this young chap's choice
I couldn't understand <u>all</u> the Spanish, but the word "broccoli" was definitely voiced.
There were also several slices of dry brown bread on a separate plate
And to the side a pile of spinach – Popeye loved it; many others hate.

A handsome, fit young man; tall, dark and incredibly
lean
So obviously for him it worked, to choose to eat so
clean.
To me it seemed a strange choice, but perhaps he is a
veggie
Well if it makes me trim like him – I'll try having
broccoli for my brekkie!

It was as if again my poems reflected the new, more rounded me; the me that was more aware of life in general; the new, different me. After the death of my dad, there was no more dearth of my poetry. What else was to come?

Delightening

Poems were continuing to appear, and one particular morning I got woken up in the early hours with another fully-formed poem. It's called "The Myth of the Welsh Dragon". One reason I think it's one of my best so far is because I'm not a true Welsh woman. Despite having lived all my life in Wales, I was born in England to English parents. I believe this poem is pretty good because it has been described by someone who is a first language Welsh speaker as well and truly Welsh and captures Welshness perfectly. This one excited me because, for the first time, I thought this was a poem that could be sold, that perhaps people would buy. I felt it could be an actual commercial poem.

There were also some beautiful new synchronicities attached to this poem. I had met a guiding light. He was one of my foot care clients and had been telling me about a book he had written, and we got chatting about my writing. This gentleman truly was a "light" because that was his nature and also his surname! He very generously asked to read some of my offerings. Bear in mind that even though I had now written over 100 poems, I had kept them under wraps and hadn't shared them with anyone except my parents and my partner.

I told him about this poem and how I could visualise it, how I wanted to sell it and give some proceeds to charities and ultimately would love to see it as a short, animated film and book narrated by Michael Sheen (well I can dream, can't I?) It's incredible where some random conversations can take us, or are they indeed random? A week or so later, an email landed in my inbox with my poem beautifully illustrated by this lovely gentleman. I had no idea that he was an artist and had illustrated his own book, not just written it. So, thank you, Brian Light, for the gift of your illustrations. I have even more gratitude to offer this man because it is down to him that I first started writing this book.

The few friends and family that I had shared some of my poems with had been telling me that I should be publishing them in a book, but I didn't think they were good enough and always said that I wouldn't buy a poetry book, so I couldn't imagine why anyone else would. Over a cuppa and cake, Brian and I were discussing this, and he asked me what my story was and when and why had I started writing poems. I found myself telling him about how they had started following my divorce and subsequent depression, and he said: "Well then, there's your story". He made me feel it needed to be written, to be seen, to be heard. He gave me the confidence to start. It was another occurrence that contributed to my belief that everything happens for a reason.

And so I began writing this book. It has been cathartic, enlightening, healing and releasing. As I have retraced my steps through my trauma, I have found very deep-seated, hidden emotions unveiling themselves. Some were surprising; some weren't, but all of it has been good for me, and I would urge anyone who has been through any trauma to just start writing about them. Getting my thoughts and feelings down on paper has given them wings. It released them from being trapped inside and thus freed me up enormously. It also gave me emotions and issues for me to follow up on and release using energy kinesiology.

If you decide to write down your feelings and thoughts, what you do with those words then is up to you. One option is to burn them and let them go. Another is to publish them, like me, in the hope that your story might help someone else heal. Or perhaps you might consider sharing your words with the person or people involved, which may help them understand your point of view, or it may help you all heal if this is safe to do so. Maybe you just write to get the words out of your head and your body to free yourself from them. Words are so powerful, whether written, spoken, read or sung. Words have energy, and if you'd like to investigate this further, take a look at Dr Masaru Emoto's work. It shows the effect negative and positive words have on water. His books *Messages from Water 1 and 2* are very interesting and incredibly enlightening.

Writing about this part of my life has opened up a whole new world for me where further synchronicities have occurred. I have come across local writing and creative groups where I have made some wonderful new friends and connected with some extremely special people. I am being stretched and am growing in a completely different direction, one I had never dreamed of. I have now written a couple of pieces of prose which is something I shall continue to explore. I was told that I have the makings of a scriptwriter, which I have yet to explore, and I have gained confidence in delivering my poems verbally to groups such as the Women's Institute and at Poems and Pints evenings. I have been interviewed for a few podcasts, and I would love to do more public speaking and presenting of my poems. Several have been set to visuals and are available to view online.

I have no idea where any of this may be going, and that in itself is exciting and interesting, and I love it. I adore this newfound lease of life that I have been gifted with, which I wouldn't have had if I had chosen to drive off the Beacons all those years ago.

Life is so precious, and time goes by so quickly, so it's all the more important that we seize opportunities and make the most of this one chance we get. We must make the most of our "snowflake catching opportunities".

To Catch a Snowflake

To catch a snowflake is so hard
One touch and then it's gone
Life it seems is similar
It doesn't last too long.

Years just rush on past us
All of a sudden, we're getting old
It quietly creeps up on you
It's a bit like catching a cold.

So much advice on how to live
Come on "live life for today!"
It's what we keep on being told
Hard to do, but easy to say!

"Life" it seems, "is for living"
And we only get one chance
So while no-one is watching
Get up and have a dance.

"Sing like no-one can hear you"
"Love like you have never before"
All these clichés surround us
But do we really know the score?

Think about it, do you live to work?
'Cause life does get in the way
Or do you really work to live
And forget work at the end of the day?

Families bring some burdens
Decisions, debts or worse
So why not give yourself a break
At times just put yourself first?

Don't bang your head on that brick wall
Why not seize the day?
Just try and catch a snowflake
From those that drift your way.

To me, they're opportunities
So seize them before they're gone.
Risk getting caught in a snowstorm
'Cause chances aren't around for long.

The choice is yours of how you live
Is each day such a bind?
Go and chase some snowflakes
Laugh at the daily grind.

So perhaps it is all perception
The way we view our fate
For me, it is a challenge.
For you? Well it's never too late!

To catch a snowflake is so hard
One touch and then it's gone
Life it seems is similar
Don't forget, we're not here long!

_____

Epilogue

Life, as we know it, has changed and not necessarily for the better. The world has been hit by a pandemic which has affected everyone. One of the first things I did when we came out of the initial lockdown was to go and visit my mum. The feeling of freedom to travel was heightened and made more poignant because of all the restrictions. I felt so excited to be finally going home and seeing my lovely mum in reality rather than through a flat computer screen.

I was blessed with gorgeous weather, which enhanced the feeling of joy and gratitude in my heart. It was a delight to be out on the open road in the stunning scenery of Mid Wales. Elements of this journey have changed since I first used to drive through the beautiful Brecon Beacons back and forth to polytechnic in the early 1980s, and these are reflected in this poem.

The fundamentals have remained the same. Over the years, I had taken them for granted and driven through with barely a cursory glance, but their strength, power and magnificence are still there in all their glory. Over the intervening years, I have become aware of a strong spiritual feeling deep inside whenever I drive across, and I really drink these feelings in. I connect with my spiritual guides much more easily when I'm in the mountains. Could I have picked up on these energies without knowing it each time I drove through? Could they have been there all along, and especially that day I didn't kill myself? Over the years, many elements of myself have changed too, but did the Beacons share its fundamentals with me and have they been inside me all along? Now there's a thought!

I am now so aware and more appreciative of how their crevasses resemble deep wrinkles on the faces of their slopes. The gradual sweep of the hillsides mirrors the shape of the wild Welsh ponies' necks that roam the mountains.

Throughout the seasons, there are various shades, hues and tones of colour. In autumn, we are shown earthy bracken browns and tans. The winter brings the glistening white of the snow and ice, together with the greys of the underlying rocks that poke through, creating such a marked contrast. In summer, there are a plethora of greens, and in spring, the heather adds purples to the seasonal palette mix.

At various times these colours are dotted with the off-white, black and sometimes chocolate colours of the many sheep that graze these hills – as they have done for time immemorial. In more recent times, blacks, tans, whites, creams and greys of ponies and cattle punctuate the vista. Occasionally the camouflage of the Army can actually be seen as they practice their manoeuvres - the men weighed down heavily by their huge backpacks as if carrying the weight of the world on their shoulders.

The weather can change in seconds from clear but perhaps gloomy skies to being plunged into thick fog or drizzly mists where you can barely see a yard ahead. After rainy days, of which there are many, there are torrents of water whooshing down from the mountains via waterfalls and streams and during a heatwave (yes, we do have these in Wales), they dry up like skin that hasn't seen moisturiser for months.

I love these mountains. I love the strong, powerful, magnificent energy of them. I love how they make me feel alive. They bring a depth of feeling and range of emotions to my soul. The 360° views from the top of Pen y Fan or Corn Ddu on a clear day are breathtaking, and the air is so light and so fresh. I adore the feeling of freedom and happiness invoked in me when driving through them, with the huge open skies above and the wide valley below leading the eye towards the Black Mountains.

I often stop to watch or photograph the Red Kites in wonder and awe as they glide and circle high up, intent only on their prey, their tail feathers adjusting the angle to deal with the ever-changing wind direction. I have seen stallions fighting and sadly many dead sheep by the side of the road - a sight that always brings sadness to my heart.

I feel amazed whenever I see the brightly coloured lycra-clad cyclists and wonder how on earth they climbed the steep roads to reach such heights. I think to myself that they must have thighs of steel. I get a bit fearful when motorcyclists whizz by at ridiculous speeds; scared for them, for myself and other road users. They have so little protection and seemingly so little care for their own lives or the effect they have on others. I am reminded of how fragile life is when I see memorials on the side of the road.

These mountains are part of my life – a huge part of my life. The roads that wend their way around the sides of these mountains have been my way home for a long time. They lead me to the safety, security and comfort of my family. They guide me back to where I belong, to where I grew up. They lead me home. I feel as though every inch of the roads from South to Mid Wales is etched in my memory. I'm sure every car I have ever had would be able to find its own way. I believe perhaps I would be able to drive the route blindfold without driving over the edge.

There used to be a time when I wouldn't see another living soul. They used to be deserted, but gradually over the intervening years, their secret has been discovered. More and more people have been drawn to the Beacons to experience the freedom of the outdoors in these beautiful surroundings. I like to think of them as Beacons of Hope. I feel they saved me and gave me hope.

The Beautiful Brecon Beacons

The beautiful Beacons still beckon me home
Now more walkers and hikers on the hillsides do roam.
There's a new speed limit of 30 miles an hour
On weekends; for drivers it sure makes them glower.
Motorbikes buzz round the cars like big angry bees
Riders leaning over on bends almost scraping their knees.
The cyclists often ride more than two abreast
But sometimes pull in if they're in need of a rest.
I still love the drive through my happy place
Especially in the sunshine - it puts a smile on my face.
The scenery over years has so barely changed
They are still magnificent - they're MY mountain range.

I spend a lot of time reflecting on life when I'm driving over the Beacons. The drive gives me space for my mind to roam, and I find myself connecting to energies and being more in touch with myself. I get time to just be, to appreciate the natural beauty and wonder of this planet that we live on. I am reminded of how grateful I am to still be living.

This gratitude to still be here, together with a poem written by Meggie Royer called "The Morning After I Killed Myself", inspired me to write a poem to celebrate all the reasons that I am grateful to be here. When I heard her poem, it affected and touched me deeply. That poem shone a spotlight on the fact that I am still here and lucky to be so, when others aren't. It also made me realise that I had not actually given much attention to my suicidal thought - to that specific instant when those words spoke to me, urging me to drive over the edge of the mountain.

I had spent so much time working on getting myself out of depression and learning to live again that I hadn't inspected the thought itself or that actual moment, nor given gratitude to the fact that

I did not act upon that thought. On hearing Meggie's poem, I was instantly moved to tears, and it induced a deluge of emotion that night and the following day. This outpouring was accompanied by the appearance of my poem of celebration and gratitude for the fact that I am still here and I'm thriving.

That poem I wrote led to this book title being born; another reason I am grateful that I am still here and that I am alive. There is life after divorce, there is happiness after thoughts of suicide, there is light at the end of the dark tunnel of depression, there is delightenment to be found and reasons to celebrate and make the most of this one precious life we are all gifted with.

If I had driven over the side of the mountain, I wouldn't have written this book and decided to delve deeper to release my demons. I wouldn't have been around to experience the life I have had, to learn to love myself, and I certainly wouldn't have been in a position to help others.

Whether it was me that chose life or whether life chose me, I'm so thankful that I am still here to celebrate it and explore possibilities and create opportunities. I feel blessed to have been able to make the most of everything that has come my way and to have had the experiences mentioned in my celebratory poem: **"The Day I Didn't Kill Myself"**.

The Day I Didn't Kill Myself

I once heard a *Meggie Royer* poem
That stopped me dead in my tracks
It hit my heart and halted my breath
And re-wound my memory back.

"The Morning After I Killed Myself"
In its simplicity, is so strong
It transported me back to my suicidal thought
After my whole world had gone wrong.

What if I had actually done it?
Performed and executed my thought
Think of all the things I would have missed
And all the grief, this end would have brought.

I would no longer see the sun rise or set
Or gaze in awe at the silvery moon
Or guess shapes in the clouds as they floated by
Because I would have been gone too soon.

No more time to just sit and ponder
Nor meditate in the peace and the quiet
Bend and stretch my body in yoga
Or wonder whether I should go on a diet.

I wouldn't have broken an arrow with my neck
Nor walked over extremely hot coals
Or realised that everything is energy
Nor achieved any more of my goals

I would never have sung on a stage
Or even believed that I ever could
I couldn't have become a tree hugger
Whenever I walked through the wood.

I wouldn't have had any more fun
Or know what pottery clay's like to hold
Or laughed when it fell off the wheel
Or known what it would be like to get old.

I wouldn't have met my nephews and niece
Felt their soft downy heads with my finger
Or seen them grow up over the years
Because I decided to no longer linger.

I would never have written any poems
Or discovered that I do have a voice
Or realise that our journey has a start and an end
But in between that we all have a choice.

I would never have seen this virus appear
And wonder what living really means
To look at my reflection in the mirror
And decide I must follow my dreams.

Lately my growth has accelerated
As a result of me writing this book
It's uncovered feelings buried deeply
I'm ready now to do more than just look.

If I'd gone I wouldn't have found new passions
And special people to help unfold my wings
To bring my words out into the open
I'm so grateful to have unearthed these things.

I suppose my recovery truly began
The second I chose to stay on that road
An awakening seemed to occur within
Though it appeared to be written in code.

Each day since has uncovered so much
It's been interesting, exciting and more
I'm so looking forward to the rest of my life
And loving who I am at my core.

Meggie's poem hit me right between the eyes
And brought up many a tear
Because it reminded me: I DID NOT KILL MYSELF
And I'm overjoyed that I am still here.

———————————————————————

Thank You

In memory of Dad up in heaven, who was always there alongside Mum, solidly supporting me all my life and to whom I attribute my innate cheerfulness and optimism. I chose my writer's name of DebS as a tribute to him (as the capital S is the first letter of his surname.) Cheers, Dad.

To my three lovely brothers who are there whenever I need them; I want you to know this works both ways.

I would not have been able to get through this chapter of my life without the support of many other beautiful humans who were there for either a reason, a season or a lifetime. There are too many to name individually. You know what part you played in my life and in my recovery, and for that, I sincerely thank you.

There are also key people who appeared in my life when I really needed them and deserve a specific mention as they triggered either a new start or a new direction.

In order of appearance:

Roger B; for the good times and without us following separate future paths, I would never have had the pleasure of discovering what I am really made of, of knowing who I could become and the gift of learning to love myself.

Dr Annie P: a wonderful GP and human being.

Megan R: amazing counsellor and friend.

John W: phenomenal energy healer who is sadly no longer with us. He opened my mind to see more than just a physical body needing therapy.

Sandy E: whose "witchy" intuition pointed me in the right direction several times.

Dave L: for incredible generosity in financing the poetry booklet, without which I would not have seen another side of Chris.

Chris H J: for holding my hand and walking alongside me on the latter part of this journey. For helping mend my heart and for having the gift of making me laugh – a lot!

Brian L: who is no longer with us. Thank you for giving me my starting point and gifting me the illustrations for my poem "The Myth of the Welsh Dragon".

A huge thank you to the cheerleaders, beta readers and those who shared their wisdom and knowledge of this brand new world of writing to me and to all the people who have encouraged, supported, motivated and inspired me to write and publish this book.

And last but not least, a huge thank you to you, the reader, for taking the time to read this book. I hope there was something in it that you could take away and that serves you well.

I believe that people come into our lives for a reason, season or a lifetime and I am truly grateful for every single one that has been, gone, is still here or yet to come.

Free Gift

As a thank you for buying this book
scan the following QR code,
then click "open website"
for a relaxing breathing exercise
I have recorded for you:

Further Inspiration

If you would like to:

- sign up for my mailing list for offers, events, future books or poems
- find information and links for many of the treatments and techniques that contributed to my recovery
- discover more about treatments I offer that could help you
- order a frameable A4 copy of the poem: "The Myth of the Welsh Dragon"

visit: www.supersonicself.com

or email: hello@supersonicself.com

About the Author

Imagine meeting up with DebS for a walk in nature where she is waiting for you by a path leading into a beautiful forest. You feel a warmth and joy radiating from her as she waves excitedly at you. Her eyes are sparkling from underneath the bobble hat and her smile, which lights up her face, seems to emanate from deep within.

You walk together down the path, where wide oaks and tall silver birches are listening to your conversation. Occasionally she puts her finger to her lips and bids you to be still and quiet as she stops to take a photograph of something she has spotted such as a bird, butterfly, shapes of branches or shadows of leaves. Photography is clearly one of her passions.

You feel comfortable in her calming presence. She is as curious about you as you might be about her but would prefer for you to speak first because she loves hearing about other people's lives.

When you ask her about her path in life, she tells you that she has always loved words and has a treasured photo of herself in bed surrounded by books at the tender age of about three or four. So you find it surprising that it wasn't until the late 1990s when she first started writing and that her writing came in the form of rhyming poems. It was clearly both a shock and surprise to her as she felt she was "channelling" them; they certainly didn't feel as if they were coming from her head.

She goes on to say that her journey of writing this book has been an exploration of herself and that this is perhaps one of the greatest gifts she has been given and is probably the best gift we can give ourselves.

"To expand and grow, to be the best version of ourselves we can be, for me meant delving deeper than I had ever done before and releasing so many self-sabotaging, limiting patterns that were restricting me. I'm not saying it's an easy path, but I truly believe that many of our energies can make us stuck or get stuck within our bodies or our auras, and if we don't get our energy back into flow, then neither ourselves nor our lives will feel particularly great!"

Momentarily distracted, she points up to the sky. *"Listen, can you hear that?"* A couple of buzzards are circling high up, carried on the thermals, their cries sounding like babies, clashing with the sweet birdsong coming from the trees. She says: *"Pick a tree and lean against it or hug it if you prefer. Take a deep breath and tune in. Isn't nature wonderful? It reminds me to be grateful that I'm still here on this magnificent planet of ours. I feel so blessed."*

After some quiet reflection, she says: "And now we have replenished our souls, how about replenishing our bodies with a well-earned cup of tea and homemade piece of cake?"

In the cafe, she takes off her hat, which reveals a blonde mane interspersed with her latest hair colour choice. She laughs and tells of a couple of times when she has had a whole rainbow of colour in her hair. It makes you smile when she suddenly breaks into song, singing along and tapping her fingers to a song in the background. As you discuss books, music, hobbies and life in general, you feel listened to and heard.

When you say goodbye, you feel you've made a new connection – whether for a reason, a season or a lifetime. DebS envelops you in a lovely big hug before heading home.

NB: As you can see, DebS didn't want this to be the usual list of facts. She wanted to give you a flavour of DebS, the person and this is a mere sip!

Printed in Great Britain
by Amazon